To:

_____

From:

_____

Date:

_____

Originally published under the title: *Experiencing God Every Day of the Year Perpetual Calendar* by Henry T. Blackaby and Claude V. King. Compiled by Trent Butler. Original product is no longer available from the publisher.

© 1995 by B & H Publishing Group, 127 Ninth Avenue North, Nashville, TN 37234

© 2009 Christian Art Gifts, RSA
        Christian Art Gifts Inc., IL, USA

Designed by Christian Art Gifts

Scripture quotations are taken from the *Holy Bible,* New King James Version, copyright © 1979, 1980, 1982 by Thomas Nelson, Inc., Publishers. Used by permission.

Images used under license from Shutterstock.com

Printed in China

ISBN 978-1-77036-237-6

10 11 12 13 14 15 16 17 18 19 – 13 12 11 10 9 8 7 6 5 4

Day by Day
with GOD

Henry Blackaby
Claude V. King

christian
art gifts ®

January

I will carry you! I have made, and I will bear;
I will carry, and will deliver you. ~ Isaiah 46:4

God Works in Creation

God saw everything that He had made,
and indeed it was very good.

~ Genesis 1:31

God revealed Himself at work the first day of creation. His crowning work in creation was the divine decision to form human beings for a love relationship with Himself.

Thank You, Creator God, for making me and my world and for continuing to work so that I may experience You. I give You my life in obedience today so I may see the work You continue to do in Your creation. Amen.

January 1

God's Love Relationship
with All His Creation

The LORD God formed man of the dust of the ground,
and breathed into his nostrils the breath of life;
and man became a living being.

~ Genesis 2:7

Love prompted God to create you and your world. You are the result of God's choice to love. He wants a relationship with you like the one He had with Adam and Eve in the Garden of Eden: to walk with you each moment in a way that you never want to hide from Him.

God, help me this day to show how much I love You as I join in Your work. Today, let me see signs of Your great love for me in the world You created. Amen.

January 2

God Invites You
to Work with Him

The LORD God took the man and put him
in the garden of Eden to tend and keep it.

~ Genesis 2:15

In creation's first week, God invited Adam and Eve to join Him in working in the garden. Creation is not finished and God has work for you. When He shows you where He is working, you have received your invitation from Him to go to work with Him.

God, I confess that I am not where You want me to be. Open up the glories of Your creation that I may see You at work and recognize Your invitation to join in. Amen.

January 3

God Speaks Through Creation

Out of the ground the LORD God made every tree
grow that is pleasant to the sight and good for food.

~ Genesis 2:9

God's first work produced beauty, beauty that speaks through the grandeur of silence about who He is. Only as God speaks do we know Him, His purposes, and His ways.

Lord God, maker of heaven and earth, You have chosen to speak with me so You can have a love relationship with me. Open my ears, my eyes, my heart so that I may hear You speak. Amen.

A Crisis of Belief

The LORD God commanded the man, saying,
"Of every tree of the garden you may freely eat, but
of the tree of the knowledge of good and evil you shall
not eat, for in the day that you eat of it you shall surely die."
~ Genesis 2:16-17

When God reveals what He wants to do, you will face a crisis of belief. He does God-sized work and calls you to do the same. Without God's help, you will fail, like Adam and Eve in the garden. Your response to the crisis of belief determines whether you will experience God.

Almighty, only Your work is important in this world, but Your work is so God-sized. I cannot do any part of it by myself. Show me the work You are doing that I can be a part of. May I have faith to begin the work. Amen.

January 5

Life Adjustments After the Fall

The LORD God sent him out of the garden of Eden
to till the ground from which he was taken.

~ Genesis 3:23

When God spoke to people in the Scripture about something He wanted to do through them, they had to adjust their lives to God. Sin in Eden showed this pattern. Adam and Eve deserved immediate death but God called them to new work. Outside Eden, they began a family and recognized God at work in the miracle of birth.

Forgiving God, show me the plan You have
for my life. I do not want to be so satisfied with
present routine that I miss Your voice. Give me
faith to go where You are working. Amen.

January 6

Obey and Experience
God in Blessing

God blessed them, and God said to them,
"Be fruitful and multiply; fill the earth and subdue it;
have dominion over the fish of the sea, over the birds of the air,
and over every living thing that moves on the earth."

~ Genesis 1:28

God's blessing for Adam and Eve was an invitation to join in His work; having a family, caring for creation, and organizing the creatures of the world. Only a world where God blesses with work, and people respond in obedience, is a very good world.

God, as You bless me with Your work to do, place in me a heart of obedience. Encourage me as I find You at work and seek to obediently answer Your invitation. Amen.

January 7

God Works Amidst Evil

The LORD said to him, "Therefore, whoever kills Cain, vengeance shall be taken on him sevenfold." And the LORD set a mark on Cain, lest anyone finding him should kill him.

~ Genesis 4:15

Cain thought his sin and the life adjustment God called him to meant the end of a relationship with God. Lovingly, God worked with Cain to protect him and show him new life possibilities. Because you once raised Cain does not mean you can no longer experience God.

Understanding Father, You know I have sinned and failed You. Make clear to me once more that You are at work and still inviting me to join in. Forgive my sin. Amen.

January 8

God's Love Relationship
Despite Evil

Noah found grace in the eyes of the Lord.

~ Genesis 6:8

All the sin in the world does not stop God from seeking for someone who wants a love relationship with Him. A love relationship with God is more important than any other single factor in your life.

God of grace, be merciful to me, a sinner lost in the flood of the world's evil. Forgive my sin. I claim Your promises and enter this moment into the love relationship You want to have with me. Amen.

January 9

God Invites You
to Overcome Evil

*"Make yourself an ark of gopherwood; make rooms in
the ark, and cover it inside and outside with pitch."*

~ *Genesis 6:14*

When you see the Father at work around you, that
is your invitation to join Him in that work. The
principle seems easy enough, but what happens
when God's work contradicts all human reason?

Do not decide whether God is at work by using
human reason. Human reason got us into the evil
that threatens our world. Only superhuman, divine
reason can get us out. What kind of ark building
does God want you to do?

*Your reason is far beyond my limited capacities.
Give me courage to go against human opinion
and fight evil the way You are fighting it. Amen.*

January 10

God Speaks as You Obey

*Then the L*ORD *said to Noah, "Come into the ark,*
you and all your household, because I have seen that
you are righteous before Me in this generation."

~ Genesis 7:1

God accomplishes His goals through people whose obedience has prepared them to do the work God is ready to do. Noah stood out above all the crowd for God to see. Do you look so much like the crowd that God must turn elsewhere to do His work?

Righteous God, I want to obey You and be
prepared to do Your work. Speak to my heart
today. I will step out of the crowd to join
You in Your work of redemption. Amen.

January 11

Superhuman Reasoning

So the LORD said, "I will destroy man whom I have created
from the face of the earth, both man and beast, creeping thing
and birds of the air, for I am sorry that I have made them."

~ *Genesis 6:7*

Noah faced a crisis of belief where he had to decide what he believed about God. Could he believe in a God whose purpose was to destroy all creation? Human reason said, run, hide. Faith said, listen, obey. To which voice do you listen?

You are beyond my understanding. Part of
me wants to turn one way. Another part
wants to turn the other. Help me, Lord.
I want to exercise faith. I will obey You. Amen.

Against the Crowd

Thus Noah did; according to all that
God commanded him, so he did.

~ Genesis 6:22

Many of us want God to give us an assignment. However, we are not interested in making any major adjustments in our lives. You must listen to God speak and do things His way. God builds arks. Arks are lonely places, standing away from and against the crowd. Are you ready to let God's love relationship be your only relationship?

Lover of my soul, I want You and You alone.
I will change my life however You indicate and will
go against the crowd. Take me away from all
wickedness and into Your perfect love. Amen.

Obey and Experience God in Covenant Promise

"Thus I establish My covenant with you: Never again shall all flesh be cut off by the waters of the flood; never again shall there be a flood to destroy the earth."

~ Genesis 9:11

Covenant is the deepest level God has chosen to reveal Himself. In covenant, God makes a promise to you and calls on you to trust Him to keep that promise. Obey Him.

Covenant Maker, I come to You only as a covenant breaker. Life in this world lets me forget Your promises and ignore Your invitations. Forgive me. Thank You for making covenants with me and letting me obey and experience You. Amen.

January 14

God Works Where You Least Expect

Abram was very rich in livestock, in silver, and in gold.

~ Genesis 13:2

All the persons you see in Scripture were ordinary people. It was their relationship with God that made them extraordinary. God's work in blessing Abraham came only after His work of bringing Abraham into a loving, faith relationship that called for major life adjustments. Only God would have chosen Abraham.

Extraordinary God, thank You for loving ordinary people like me. Give me extraordinary faith to join in Your extraordinary work. Amen.

A Love Relationship with God

"I will establish My covenant between Me and you and your descendants after you in their generations, for an everlasting covenant, to be God to you and your descendants after you."

~ Genesis 17:7

Abraham answered God's call to mission. In answering the call, Abraham found himself called into a love relationship with God that would affect the entire world forever. You, too, can have everlasting influence. Will you join Him in His everlasting work?

Eternal God, show me the way my life fits into Your everlasting plan. Thank You for loving me so much that You created a plan for my life. Amen.

January 16

God Invites You on
an Unknown Mission

Now the LORD had said to Abram: "Get out of your country, from your family and from your father's house, to a land that I will show you."

~ *Genesis 12:1*

The call to relationship is also a call to be on mission with God. That call to mission disrupts your entire life. As you listen for God's invitation, know its destiny is always: Point Unknown. Are you willing to go?

Lord of destinies, You know where and how my life fits best into Your plan. Do not let worldly dreams rob me of eternal destinies. Amen.

God Speaks When You Fear

*After these things the word of the L*ORD *came to Abram in a vision, saying, "Do not be afraid, Abram. I am your shield, your exceedingly great reward."*

~ *Genesis 15:1*

To understand your bad or difficult circumstances, God's perspective is vital. Deep trouble and crisis is often the easiest time to hear God speak. One word He always gives in such situations, "Do not be afraid." Fear is the human reaction to problems. Hope is God's reaction.

You who takes away all fear, look in love on me today. You know the circumstances that bring fear, frustration, and failure to my life. Only Your word can dispel my fears and deepen my hope. Amen.

January 18

The Faith Crisis

*But Abram said, "Lord G*OD*, what will You give me, seeing I go childless, and the heir of my house is Eliezer of Damascus?"*

~ Genesis 15:2

The life of faith is not a life without questions. Abraham heard God's promises but saw no way they could be fulfilled since he had no son. Such a crisis could bring resignation. For faith, such a crisis brings new conversations and new answers.

Father of hope, renew my hope in You. I have tough questions to ask You, for I do not understand many things. Wrestling in prayer renews hope and allows me to walk afresh the path of faith. Amen.

January 19

Surrender the Promise

So Abraham rose early in the morning and saddled his donkey, and took two of his young men with him, and Isaac his son; and he split the wood for the burnt offering, and arose and went to the place of which God had told him.

~ Genesis 22:3

Abraham found that adjustments and obedience were costly. God said, "Give me the son." The Bible mentions none of Abraham's feelings, only the life adjustment he was willing to make. He heard the Word and acted on it. That is faith; that is obedience; that is experiencing God.

Father of the fathomless future, I am willing to surrender the promise as I see it in order to gain the promise as You give it. I will adjust my life to Yours. Amen.

January 20

Obey and Experience
God Through His Open Door

And He said, "Do not lay your hand on the lad, or do anything to him; for now I know that you fear God, since you have not withheld your son, your only son, from Me."

~ Genesis 22:12

Human will and reason does not sacrifice an only son, especially a son of promise. Such work is God-sized, done by God's presence in you. In joining God in such work, you intimately experience God and life is never again the same. What God-sized experiences are changing your life?

God, You work in ways beyond my imagination. Often Your work seems to make no sense and even seems to contradict what I have learned about You before. Help me to adjust my life and achieve an experience of obedience with You. Amen.

January 21

God Works Among Human Deception

When the LORD saw that Leah was unloved,
He opened her womb; but Rachel was barren.

~ Genesis 29:31

Jacob was constantly about his own business. God constantly worked in different areas. Only God-sized work made Jacob, the temperamental deceiver, open to God's work. That means God has hope for you.

Lord of hope, too often I consider myself hopeless.
Forgive me for giving up on You as You work in me.
Raise my sights from what I want and what I can
accomplish, to what You want and what You
are planning to accomplish. Amen.

January 22

God's Love for You
When You Do Not Love

Esau ran to meet him, and embraced him,
and fell on his neck and kissed him, and they wept.

~ *Genesis 33:4*

Jacob deceived and cheated his brother, Esau, until his brother became the feared enemy. Long years in exile, experiencing God's love and seeing God at work, finally changed Jacob. What fears, hatreds, and broken relationships does God want to heal through His love relationship with you?

God, You are love. I seem to be hatred. Every time
I try to love someone, I find myself creating a new
barrier of distrust, of fear, of hate. Entwine me in
Your love so enemies become beloved. Amen.

January 23

God Invites the
Deceiver into His Home

"I am the God of Bethel, where you anointed the pillar
and where you made a vow to Me. Now arise, get out of
this land, and return to the land of your family."

~ Genesis 31:13

Having alienated his family, Jacob fled. He met God in a dream and named the place Bethel, "house of God."

When God prepared Jacob to return home, God introduced Himself again as "the God of Bethel," flooding Jacob with warm memories. God often invites us by reminding us of past love experiences with Him. What reminder is He giving you today?

Thank You for the memories You are bringing to my mind of our love relationship together. Let me see from the past Your present invitation to the future. Amen.

January 24

God Speaks in Human Relationships

"It is in my power to do you harm, but the God of your father spoke to me last night, saying, 'Be careful that you speak to Jacob neither good nor bad.'"

~ *Genesis 31:29*

God's divine word intervened in Laban's plans for revenge on Jacob. God's Word mended broken family relationships and gave Jacob freedom to continue on his way in answer to God's invitation. Is God trying to speak to you even through your broken relationships?

Father, I have let sin and forgetfulness break important relationships in my life. Forgive me. Speak to me even through those I have hated, deceived, and ignored. Amen.

January 25

A Crisis of Faith
when Facing Death

Now it came to pass, when she was in hard labor, that the midwife said to her, "Do not fear; you will have this son also."

~ *Genesis 35:17*

Human loyalties may blur God's voice from us. Certainly, mixed emotions flowed through Jacob as he knew at the same time Rachel was giving him a son, death was robbing him of his beloved wife.

What life crisis threatens to rob you of human loyalties and support? How is this a crisis of faith for you? What is your response?

Why, God, did You build crisis and loss into life and love relationship with You? I do not understand the circumstances I face. Help me, Lord. Be present with me. Calm my fears. Amen.

January 26

Life Adjustments

And Jacob set a pillar on her grave,
which is the pillar of Rachel's grave to this day.

~ Genesis 35:20

Adjusting your life to God is a critical turning point in knowing and doing the will of God. Death says, "Stay here. Remember." Faith says, "Face the new life situation. Make the adjustments God calls for."

What past grabs you and robs you of God's future for you? How must you adjust in order to join in what God is doing?

Father of all my futures, I am stuck in the past.
I do not know how to let it go and move on. I must
adjust my life to Your future. Show me how. Amen.

Obey and Experience
God without Fear

And he built an altar there and called the
place El Bethel, because there God appeared to him
when he fled from the face of his brother.

~ Genesis 35:7

The reward for obedience and love is that God will reveal Himself. Finally, Jacob learned that lesson and his relationship to God became all important. Again he returned to Bethel. This time he knew what was important. God appeared there. He experienced God there. All other priorities vanished in the breeze. Have you received God's reward?

Awesome One whose very presence is fearsome,
remove the fears that make me seek worldly ways
and worldly rewards. Implant in me the desire
to know You and nothing else. Amen.

January 28

God Works Among Children

His brothers envied him, but his
father kept the matter in mind.

~ Genesis 37:11

God is always at work but we have problems believing it. Too many excuses pop up, "I am not good enough. I do not obey well enough." Joseph had the most logical excuse. He was too young.

God surprised him with dreams, dreams that divided his family into two camps. How do you respond to God at work? With envy? With doubt? With a will to join Him?

You chose to bring all of us, even Your Son,
into the world as children. Surely You will not
ignore us until we reach a certain age. Give me faith
to do the work You have sent me to do. Amen.

What's Your Purpose?

Joseph said to them, "Do not be afraid, for am I in the place of God? But as for you, you meant evil against me; but God meant it for good, in order to bring it about as it is this day, to save many people alive."

~ Genesis 50:19-20

Joseph's brothers feared the past would find them out. They thought revenge dominated Joseph. Instead, God's love did. Delivering people, not dooming them, was Joseph's purpose because it was God's purpose. What is your purpose?

Take away my pessimistic fear. Replace it with the love relationship that orients all life on Your loving-purposes. I dedicate myself to Your purpose. Amen.

January 30

God Invites You
to Unlikely Places

*"Hurry and go up to my father, and say to him, 'Thus
says your son Joseph: God has made me lord of
all Egypt; come down to me, do not tarry.'"*

~ Genesis 45:9

Surely Jacob had a hard time accepting an invitation
to leave God's promised land. Had God forgotten
His promise to Abraham after only two generations?
God's invitation leads to unlikely places. Is the place
God chose causing you to ignore the invitation?

*God, You rule the world and work in all its parts.
Am I too comfortable in the one part I know so well?
Are You calling me to an unlikely place, a place
I would never imagine going? Speak to me.
Show me Your purpose. I will go. Amen.*

January 31

February

Trust in the LORD with all your heart, and lean not on your own understanding; in all your ways acknowledge Him, and He shall direct your paths. ~ Proverbs 3:5-6

God Speaks
When Others Dream

*Then Joseph said to Pharaoh, "The dreams of Pharaoh
are one; God has shown Pharaoh what He is about to do."*

~ Genesis 41:25

God sometimes speaks to us by speaking to other people. He let an Egyptian ruler receive revelation, instead of Joseph, an Israelite hero of faith. Joseph had to be content as God's interpreter. Is God trying to say something to you by what He is telling someone else?

*Ruler of the world's destiny, forgive my
arrogance in trying to limit the way You speak.
I want to know Your purpose and Your ways.
Show me however You choose. Amen.*

February 1

When Promises Are Delayed

And Joseph said to his brethren, "I am dying; but God will surely visit you, and bring you out of this land to the land of which He swore to Abraham, to Isaac, and to Jacob."

~ Genesis 50:24

God takes a long look at our history, knows the best time to act, and we may not participate in that action. Centuries separated the promise to Abraham and its fulfillment. Each generation had to wait in faith, living as if God would act today. Do you tend to give up on God's promises?

All-knowing God, Your plan is always best. Give me the faith to trust Your plan and the patience not to act on my own plan. Amen.

Accept Upward Mobility

Joseph had been taken down to Egypt. And Potiphar, an
officer of Pharaoh, captain of the guard, an Egyptian, bought
him from the Ishmaelites who had taken him down there.

~ Genesis 39:1

Joseph's life may be described in one word, "adjustment." Each time Joseph went where God led and let the experience prepare Him to obey. Eventually, the road led to what we call upward mobility. For Joseph it was a constant level of obeying. Are you aiming for upward mobility?

Architect of my life, You do not always call
to the popular and the powerful but to
the place and occasion where I can obey and
experience You. I want to make every needed
adjustment so I can obey You always. Amen.

February 3

Obey and Experience God: Restoring Broken Relationships

Israel said to Joseph, "I had not thought to see your face;
but in fact, God has also shown me your offspring!"

~ *Genesis 48:11*

If you know that God loves you, you should never question a directive from Him. It will always be right and best but you may not see the rightness and bestness for a long time.

Certainly, Jacob (Israel) gave up hope long before God revealed His best plan. The wait was worth the reward. Are you questioning something you know God said? Why?

Sovereign Lord of my life, forgive me as I doubt
and question. I will lay aside my questions,
trust Your love, and do it Your way. Amen.

February 4

God Works Through Anonymous People

The children of Israel were fruitful and increased
abundantly, multiplied and grew exceedingly
mighty; and the land was filled with them.

~ Exodus 1:7

Scripture repeatedly brings us back to anonymous people. Whole generations of Israelites lived and died without being named, but God worked through unknown people to create His nation. What does God want to create through anonymous you?

Lover of all people, I am known to You.
That means I am not anonymous. It means I can
do something important, for I can join You in
Your work. Create Your purpose through me. Amen.

God Remembers His Promises

God heard their groaning, and God remembered His covenant with Abraham, with Isaac, and with Jacob. And God looked upon the children of Israel, and God acknowledged them.

~ Exodus 2:24-25

Israel experienced God's greatest love in their greatest time of need. Your love relationship can also be strongest when you are weakest. Sometimes God shows His love for you by hearing your cries. God always remembers His covenant of love.

God of covenant love, hear my cries. I am desperate, lonely, hurting, in need of friendship, faith, and finances. The world says, give up. Instead, I want You to show up. I do love You with all my heart. Amen.

God Invites You
Despite Your Objections

"Come now, therefore, and I will send you to Pharaoh that you may bring My people, the children of Israel, out of Egypt."

~ Exodus 3:10

God is all-powerful. If He ever asks you to do something, He Himself will enable you to do it. Moses was not convinced. Surely God wanted someone other than an 80-year-old, untalented, shy, murderer and shepherd.

But God's job candidate list had no alternate names. Finally, Moses went. The rest is history. What objections should God listen to from you?

All-powerful God, I am finally convinced. You do have an invitation for me to do a God-sized job. I am not ready for it, but You are. Let's go, God. Amen.

February 7

God Speaks to Introduce Himself

God said to Moses, "I AM WHO I AM." And He said, "Thus you shall say to the children of Israel, 'I AM has sent me to you.'"

~ Exodus 3:14

God speaks when He wants to involve a person in His work. He reveals Himself in order to help the person respond in faith. What has God revealed to you about Himself? How should you respond?

Great I AM, all sufficient in Yourself, yet always seeking a love relationship by speaking to us, speak once more that I may know You, love You, serve You, and follow You. Amen.

February 8

When Your Comfort Zone Is Getting Too Comfortable

And they said to them, "Let the Lord look on you and judge, because you have made us abhorrent in the sight of Pharaoh and in the sight of his servants, to put a sword in their hand to kill us."

~ Exodus 5:21

The people of Israel feared Pharaoh more than they had faith in God. They saw God's saving mission through Moses as destroying a comfortable status quo. Are you too comfortable in the world to strike out in faith, answering God's invitation?

Judge of the world, forgive my fear of the unknown and my faith in the known. I take my hands off the worldly securities I have trusted. I place my hands in Your strong hands. Together we will accomplish Your mission. Amen.

February 9

Expect Rejection

*Moses returned to the L*ORD *and said, "L*ORD*, why have You brought trouble on this people? Why is it You have sent me? For since I came to Pharaoh to speak in Your name, he has done evil to this people; neither have You delivered Your people at all."*

~ Exodus 5:22-23

When God reveals Himself, that is your invitation to adjust your life to Him. Once you have done this, you are in a position to obey, but obedience does not promise the easy life. It goes against the world's grain and you must adjust by accepting rejection.

Why will You not let me alone? Life is tough enough without You making it rougher. But I know Your way is right. Help me stay on course when the course is tough. Amen.

Follow God's Pattern

*So the L*ORD *saved Israel that day out of the hand of the Egyptians, and Israel saw the Egyptians dead on the seashore.*

~ Exodus 14:30

God invited Moses to join Him in what He was doing to deliver Israel. He told Moses what to do, Moses obeyed, and God accomplished His purposes.

Moses and those around him came to know God more clearly and intimately. This is God's pattern that leads to experiencing God. Are you following it? Are you experiencing God and His salvation each day?

Holy Savior, You have invited me to join in Your work. I have come through the crisis of faith and made the adjustments. I am obeying You and experiencing You. Thank You. Amen.

February 11

God Works to Overcome Rejection

When He had made an end of speaking with him on Mount Sinai, He gave Moses two tablets of the Testimony, tablets of stone, written with the finger of God.

~ Exodus 31:18

The Word of God is a guide for faith and practice. Israel had a hard time learning that lesson. God patiently worked with Moses to give them His Word. The Word showed them the basic direction God wanted them to go if they were to join Him in His work of redemption. Are you letting God work through His Word to direct your life?

Author of the Holy Scriptures, use Your Word today to give direction to my life. No longer will I reject You and Your way. Amen.

February 12

God's Love Relationship Draws Life's Boundaries

*Moses took the blood, sprinkled it on the people, and said,
"This is the blood of the covenant which the LORD
has made with you according to all these words."*

~ Exodus 24:8

God sealed the love relationship with Moses at the burning bush. He sealed the relationship with Israel by making a covenant with them on the holy mountain.

The people had learned in the Exodus how much God loved them. Have you learned how much God loves you?

Redeemer God, You have given the blood of Your Son, Jesus Christ, to create a new covenant with Your people. Thank You for loving us so much that You continually define the boundaries of life with You. Amen.

February 13

God Invites You to a Covenant Commitment

"Now therefore, if you will indeed obey My voice and keep My covenant, then you shall be a special treasure to Me above all people, for all the earth is Mine."

~ *Exodus 19:5*

A love relationship with God requires that you demonstrate your love by obedience. If you have an obedience problem, you have a love problem.

God wants you to be a treasure in His hand with a mission to all other people. You can be that treasure. There's only one condition: obey His voice.

God, I renew my commitment to the covenant You made with me in the blood of Jesus. You initiated the covenant because You love me. I will keep Your covenant because I love You. Amen.

February 14

God Speaks to Reveal His Purposes

"Behold, I send an Angel before you to keep you in the way and to bring you into the place which I have prepared. Beware of Him and obey His voice."

~ *Exodus 23:20-21*

As Israel yearned to return to Egypt, God planned a way to the Promised Land. Which way would Israel choose: their way or His way? They answered not with words but with obedience. How do you answer when God shows you His purposes for you?

You have the best plan for my life. But the world helps me make my own plans for my life. Help me see how much better Your plan is. Amen.

When God Is Silent

*"Go up to a land flowing with milk and honey; for I will not
go up in your midst, lest I consume you on the way,
for you are a stiff-necked people."*

~ *Exodus 33:3*

The silence of God means that He is ready to bring
into your life a greater revelation of Himself. Israel
found God's silence too much to bear and made the
golden calf. Therefore, God allowed Israel to occupy
the land but only with silence from Him. This led
to a greater revelation of God in Exodus 34. Is God
silent in your life? Why?

*Revealer of all that I need to know, break Your
silence. I confess my sins. I repent of my sins.
Speak, Lord, Your servant is waiting. Amen.*

Life Adjustments
When Giving to God

Everyone came whose heart was stirred,
and everyone whose spirit was willing, and they
*brought the L*ORD*'s offering for the work of the tabernacle*
of meeting, for all its service, and for the holy garments.

~ Exodus 35:21

Your greatest single difficulty in following God may come at the point of the adjustment. Israel had to turn from following a golden calf to giving what they owned to make a house for God. How much of what you have are you willing to give to God?

Giver of all good gifts, accept the offering I
bring to You. Your love has stirred my heart
and changed my life. I owe everything I have
to You. Here, take what You want. Amen.

February 17

Renewing Your Love Relationship

*Then [Moses] said, "If now I have found grace in Your sight,
O Lord, let my Lord, I pray, go among us, even though
we are a stiff-necked people; and pardon our iniquity
and our sin, and take us as Your inheritance."*

~ Exodus 34:9

When Israel had disobeyed, Moses prayed for them. God forgave them, renewed His covenant with them, and promised to do an awesome thing for them. Do you need to pray for forgiveness and renew Your covenant love relationship with God?

*Loving and forgiving God, I have sinned.
I have neglected You and worshiped the world.
Forgive me, renew me, use me. Amen.*

February 18

God Works in
Worship to Forgive

The priest shall make atonement for him, for his sin that he has committed in any of these matters; and it shall be forgiven him.

~ Leviticus 5:13

The first thing God did after He firmly established Israel as His covenant people was to work to show them how to find forgiveness.

Ultimately, God worked through Jesus Christ to provide forgiveness once and for all. Do you know that forgiveness?

You are always at work to establish Your ways, the ways of forgiveness and love. Work Your miracle of forgiveness in my heart right now that I may join You in forgiving others. Amen.

Love Your Neighbor

"You shall not take vengeance, nor bear any grudge against the children of your people, but you shall love your neighbor as yourself: I am the LORD."

~ *Leviticus 19:18*

God's whole plan for the advance of the Kingdom depends on His working in real and practical ways through His personal relationship with His people.

He wants people who love Him and show that love by loving other people. Whom does God want you to love today?

Lover of all, teach me to love. Too seldom do I control my time so I can make the effort to show love to others. Make Your love real and practical in my life today. Amen.

God Invites You to Imitate Him

"You shall be holy, for I the LORD your God am holy."

~ *Leviticus 19:2*

One name defines the total experience of God, "The Holy One." He is indeed holy, unlike man who is transcendent in nature and moral purity.

Still He invites us to be like Him, to be morally pure and to represent His awesome holiness to the world. In what ways is your life holy?

Holy, awesome God, I tremble in fear to face You,
yet I know that You invite me to Your pure presence to
continue our love relationship. Let the people I see today
see the holy difference You make in my life. Amen.

God Speaks to You
to Give You Life

"You shall therefore keep My statutes and My judgments, which if a man does, he shall live by them: I am the LORD."

~ *Leviticus 18:5*

God speaks when He has a purpose in mind for your life. His purpose is to give you true life and not the imitation that the world offers. God knows what it takes to have true life. He spells out the way in His teachings and laws. Do you trust His definition of life?

Author and Creator of life, only You can know what life really is. Help me trust You to lead me to true life. Amen.

February 22

Holy or Hollow

"According to the doings of the land of Egypt, where
you dwelt, you shall not do; and according to the doings
of the land of Canaan, where I am bringing you, you shall
not do; nor shall you walk in their ordinances."

~ Leviticus 18:3

God told Israel not to follow the worldly standards of Egypt and Canaan, which only gave hollow results. Instead, God said, "Live My way, a way I have created so you can become the role models. Be My holy people." Do you have a role model? For a holy life, or a hollow one?

O Holy God, You continue to call me to a uniquely
holy life. That means I must say no to so many other
people around me and the life they offer. Help me in this
quandary! I must decide to walk with You. Amen.

Is God's Holiness Present?

*"If they confess their iniquity and the iniquity of their fathers,
with their unfaithfulness in which they were unfaithful to Me,
and that they also have walked contrary to Me."*

~ Leviticus 26:40

Whenever you identify a place where you refuse to allow God's lordship, that is a place He will go to work. Life adjustment begins by identifying where God's holiness is not present in your life. What confession does God want you to make today?

All-seeing God, You know how each part of me relates to Your divine, holy purposes. Show me my sin. I will confess it and ask You to work right there in my life so I can obey and experience You. Amen.

February 24

Obey and Experience God by Being Holy before the Holy One

"But for their sake I will remember the covenant of their ancestors, whom I brought out of the land of Egypt in the sight of the nations, that I might be their God: I am the LORD."

~ *Leviticus 26:45*

God blesses those who are obedient to Him. When Israel confessed their sin and dedicated themselves to be the holy people God wanted, God promised to renew the covenant and fulfill His promises. Have you confessed your sin?

You are a covenant-making God. You have heard the confession of sin I have made, forgiven me, and renewed our covenant love relationship. Thank You, God. What a joy to experience You as I obey You. Amen.

God Works in the Midst of Your Complaints

The LORD said to Moses, "Has the LORD's arm been shortened? Now you shall see whether what I say will happen to you or not."
~ Numbers 11:23

God listened to Israel's complaints but still provided for their needs and led them towards the Promised Land.

No matter how we see things or complain, God's arm is no shorter or weaker today than in Moses' time.

Mighty God, who has power and ability to do whatever You choose, show me the work You are doing. Increase my faith. I will seek Your perspective and not mine. I will join Your work obediently. Amen.

God's Love Relationship
Is Contagious

It shall be, if you go with us – indeed it shall be – that whatever good the LORD will do to us, the same we will do to you."

~ Numbers 10:32

In Scripture God became real and personal to people. Israel expected, in their love relationship with God, that He would do good things for them.

They promised, in turn, to do good things for the family of Moses' father-in-law. Your life also can reflect that kind of real, personal, and practical relationship as you respond to God's working in your life.

*Personal God, help me to honor Your love
by passing it on to others. Amen.*

God Invites You to Receive His Spirit

"Then I will come down and talk with you there. I will take of the Spirit that is upon you and will put the same upon them; and they shall bear the burden of the people with you, that you may not bear it yourself alone."

~ Numbers 11:17

When you are saved, you enter a love relationship with Jesus Christ – God Himself. At that point the Counselor, the Spirit of Truth, comes to take up residence in your life and He is ever present to teach you.

Spirit of God, You live within me. Take total control of my life. Lead me to share the burdens of Your people and to do the work You are doing. Amen.

February 28

God Speaks As He Chooses

*"Hear now My words: if there is a prophet among you,
I, the LORD, make Myself known to him in a vision; I speak
to him in a dream. Not so with My servant Moses; He is
faithful in all My house. I speak with him face to face."*
~ Numbers 12:6-8

Aaron and Miriam wanted an experience with God just like Moses'. However, when God speaks He wants our experience with Him to be personal and unique to us. Will you let God show you His unique way of speaking to you?

*Eternal, Holy Voice, I don't ask You to speak to
me like You did to my pastor or my best friend.
I simply ask, speak so I can know You,
Your ways, and Your purposes. Amen.*

February 29

March

"Whoever desires to save his life will lose it, but whoever loses his life for My sake will find it." ~ *Matthew 16:25*

God-sized Work or Retreat

*Nevertheless the people who dwell in the land are
strong; the cities are fortified and very large; moreover
we saw the descendants of Anak there.*

~ *Numbers 13:28*

A God-sized assignment creates a crisis point where you must decide whether you will follow God's leading. Israel facing the Promised Land is a good example of this crisis of belief.

Israel looked at the giant descendants of Anak and thought they were bigger than God. This cost forty years in God's work of conquest. Has the giant size of God's project blinded you to His power?

*Lord God Almighty! You have all power.
Nothing is impossible for You. That means
nothing is impossible for You and me together.
I will begin Your work today. Amen.*

March 1

God's Will or Human Desire

Moses made a bronze serpent, and put it on a pole;
and so it was, if a serpent had bitten anyone,
when he looked at the bronze serpent, he lived.

~ Numbers 21:9

Israel decided that they preferred life in Egypt. God sent serpents to discipline them but Moses prayed for them. God invited them to make a serpent on a pole and show their faith by looking at the serpent instead of at their desperate situation.

Those who obeyed and adjusted their lives were healed. What personal desires keep you from making the life adjustments God has called for?

King of my life, no longer will I look where my
wants direct me. I will look to see what You want
and will adjust my life to be what You want. Amen.

March 2

Trust God's Word,
Not Human Wealth

How shall I curse whom God has not cursed? And how shall I denounce whom the LORD has not denounced?

You must obey God first. Then He will accomplish His work through you. Balak offered Balaam, the prophet, large amounts of money to curse Israel.

But God said to bless Israel. After much turmoil, Balaam obeyed. Then he experienced God. Are financial goals preventing you from obeying and experiencing God?

Giver of every good gift, too often I want money and what it will buy. This leads me off the path of obedience and away from Your presence. I will surrender my claims to finances and will obey what You have invited me to do. Amen.

March 3

God's Gifts to People

Look, the LORD your God has set the land before you;
go up and possess it, as the LORD God of your fathers
has spoken to you; do not fear or be discouraged.

~ Deuteronomy 1:21

From the Red Sea to Sinai to the border of the Land of Promise, God had worked for Israel. Now God announced His next work: the gift of the land. Would Israel join in this work to receive the gift? What work has God made clear to you? What keeps you from joining in?

God of revelation, You are so clearly working in
my world. I see where You want me to join in.
I will answer the call to work beside You. Amen.

March 4

God Never Forgets You

For the LORD your God is a merciful God, He will not
forsake you nor destroy you, nor forget the covenant
of your fathers which He swore to them.

~ Deuteronomy 4:31

Israel had to lose everything they had and go into
exile before they remembered God.

Then they learned that God's mercy has no end.
He is always waiting for His beloved to come back
to Him. Will you turn back to Him?

God of mercy, I have turned to so many other
things seeking hope and satisfaction. I have
found none. Now I place my life afresh in
Your arms. Please take me back. I love You. Amen.

March 5

God Invites You When You Are Still a Sinner

Be strong and of good courage, do not fear nor be afraid of them; for the LORD your God, He is the One who goes with you. He will not leave you nor forsake you.

~ *Deuteronomy 31:6*

God's commands are expressions of His nature of love. They are for our good. You can courageously obey all that God invites you to do because He is always present with you. You can count on Him and His limitless power. What fears make you forfeit the experience of God because they make you refuse to obey Him?

God, You are the one in whose presence every person must bow in awe and fear. Why then do I bow in fear before things that are so insignificant when compared to You? I call on Your power and Your courage for my life. Amen.

March 6

God Speaks Through His Word

*He wrote on the tablets according to the first writing,
the Ten Commandments, which the Lord had spoken to
you in the mountain from the midst of the fire in the day
of the assembly; and the Lord gave them to me.*

~ Deuteronomy 10:4

God wrote the Bible for Israel, but not for Israel alone. God wrote the Bible for you. You should never have to ask, "How can God speak to me today?" The Bible is His Word. Read it. Pray about it. Find what it says to you about Him, His ways, and His purposes.

Author of Holy Scripture, I sit before Your Word. Give me the power to concentrate, the obedience to listen, and the faith to act on what You will say to me as I read. Amen.

March 7

Respond to God's Salvation

Behold I set before you today a blessing and a curse: the blessing, if you obey the commandments of the LORD your God which I command you today; and the curse, if you do not obey the commandments of the LORD your God.

~ Deuteronomy 11:26-28

If you have faith in God, you will obey Him. If you lack faith, you will not do what He wants. Each time you hear what God wants, you face the crisis: obey or disobey; receive blessing or curse. Israel eventually chose the curse. What are you choosing from God?

God of all blessings, I choose the blessing. I choose to obey You. Obedience requires Your strength and will. I choose to obey, not in my power, but in Your power. Be my strength today. Amen.

March 8

Follow God's Word or Fail

*Therefore love the stranger, for you
were strangers in the land of Egypt.*

~ Deuteronomy 10:19

God loves all the world. That is the work He is doing.
God wants you to move forward from your place of
limited love. He wants to expand your horizon as a
lover of people. Will I love everyone God loves?

*Lover of all the world, my expressions of love are so
weak. My community of love is so restricted. Forgive me
for not having the courage to love. Instill in me a love
that will not let the world go by. Amen.*

March 9

Experience God in Times of Joy

*You shall rejoice before the L*ORD *your God,*
you and your sons and your daughters, your male
and female servants, and the Levite who is within your
gates, since he has no portion nor inheritance with you.

~ *Deuteronomy 12:12*

Because you love God, obey Him. Then you will fellowship with Him and will come to know Him intimately. That affirmation will be a joyous time for you. You will want to share it with others.

You can do this in worship, a worship where you invite friends and strangers to share your joy. Describe your joy to God.

Source of all rejoicing, I never knew joy until
I experienced You in faith and obedience. Amen.

March 10

God Works to
Fulfill His Promise

"Every place that the sole of your foot will tread
upon I have given you, as I said to Moses."

~ *Joshua 1:3*

Joshua got his marching orders, "Go over the Jordan
and fulfill what I promised Moses." When you want
to know what God is doing, you may need to look
at the promises He has made. His work is fulfilling
His promises. Are you working with God at fulfilling His promises?

Faithful Fulfiller of every promise, open my
eyes to the work You are still doing to fulfill
Your promises. How can I be a servant who brings
promises to reality? Show me. Work through me.
I promise to do whatever You tell me to. Amen.

March 11

God's Love Relationship Surprises Us

So the men answered her, "Our lives for yours, if none of you tell this business of ours. And it shall be, when the LORD has given us the land, that we will deal kindly and truly with you."

~ Joshua 2:14

God's choices often surprise us. The spies must have been surprised that a Canaanite prostitute would be God's agent of deliverance for them!

In her obedience she experienced God in a kind of love relationship she had never known. Does it surprise you to realize God is pursuing a love relationship with you? Will you love Him in return?

God, You constantly surprise me with
Your love. I thank You that You love me.
Fill my life with love in return. Amen.

March 12

God Invites You
to Read His Word

This Book of the Law shall not depart from your mouth, but
you shall meditate in it day and night, that you may observe to
do according to all that is written in it. For then you will make
your way prosperous, and then you will have good success.

~ *Joshua 1:8*

Life has some land mines that can wreck your life.
God does not want you to miss out on His best,
and He does not want you to see your life wrecked.
Thus God gave you His Word.

Are you meditating on it daily to find life's fullest dimensions and avoid its wrecks?

Guide of my life, open Your Word to me today
that I may experience You and know life at its
richest and fullest. Lead me around the wrecking
crews of life. I love Your Word. Amen.

March 13

God Speaks to
Prepare You for Service

Then the Commander of the Lord's army said to Joshua,
"Take your sandal off your foot, for the place where
you stand is holy." And Joshua did so.

~ Joshua 5:15

When God spoke, the person was sure God was speaking. Joshua had no doubt. He saw a soldier and heard him speak. Joshua knew the voice was God's. Are you certain you are hearing God's voice?

Lord, make me certain beyond any doubt that I have
heard Your voice. I will tell others about the experience
with You, but I do not claim to want or need to prove
You have spoken. I do not listen to gain glory for me.
I listen so I can obey. Amen.

March 14

Show Faith During Failure

Joshua said, "Alas, Lord GOD, why have You brought
this people over the Jordan at all – to deliver us into
the hands of the Amorites, to destroy us?

~ *Joshua 7:7*

Would you tell a whole army to follow you in walking around a city, expecting the walls to fall down
when you blow some trumpets? That was a crisis of
belief for Joshua and for all, but a greater crisis came
when they lost a battle.

   Life with God is not total success. How do you
feel when you fail? How do you show faith during
failure?

Victorious God of Hosts, You have the key to victory
in every situation of life. But Lord, I am not always
victorious. Teach me to obey You and experience You as
I come through failure and come back to You. Amen.

March 15

Adjust Your Life

Therefore take careful heed to yourselves
that you love the LORD your God.

~ *Joshua 23:11*

Our tendency is to want to skip the adjustment and go from believing God to obedience. But adjustment is necessary because His ways are so different from ours.

The generation after Joshua learned this the hard way. Once they had the land, they quit listening and adjusting their lives to love God in every situation. What new situations in your life tempt you to quit adjusting your life to God's ways?

O Constant One, forgive me that I have
quit making the life adjustments You require. I
will love You, obey You, and experience You.
What adjustment need I make today? Amen.

March 16

Impossible Obedience

*Joshua said to the people, "You cannot serve the L*ORD*,
for He is a holy God. He is a jealous God; He will not
forgive your transgressions nor your sins. And the people
said to Joshua, "No, but we will serve the L*ORD*!"*

~ *Joshua 24:19, 21*

Israel wanted easy obedience, an obedience of habit
and ritual. Joshua reminded them that obedience is
impossible in human power.

Israel stood to the test. They committed themselves to faith and obedience even to a God who
punished disobedience. How committed to impossible obedience are you?

*God of the impossible, make obedience possible in
my life. I can obey only because You live in my heart.
I commit myself against all odds to obey You. Amen.*

March 17

God's Call for Leaders

When the LORD raised up judges for them, the LORD
was with the judge and delivered them out of the
hand of their enemies all the days of the judge.

~ Judges 2:18

An ordinary person is who God most likes to use. If you feel weak, limited, ordinary, you are the best material through which God can work. Deborah, Gideon, and the other judges had great reasons why God could not use them.

Time after time God surprised Israel by choosing these unexpected, unqualified people to lead them. Where does God want you as a leader?

Merciful, loving One, I see no value in myself,
but somehow You keep calling me to join in Your
work, even be a leader in Your work. I surrender
my weak self to Your strong purpose. Amen.

March 18

God's Love Relationship Gives Strength

Thus let all Your enemies perish, O LORD! But let those who love Him be like the sun when it comes out in full strength.

~ Judges 5:31

Deborah's victory song shows how convinced she was of God's love. By answering God's invitation she discovered God protected her from enemies and shone His love into her whole being to give her strength.

She could do all things because God pursued her in a love relationship. What things does God's love enable you to do?

You are the Strength of my life. You have pursued me in love and caught me even when I desperately tried to evade You. Now, at all times, You give me strength to keep on keeping on. Thank You, O my Love. Amen.

March 19

God Invites You to
Accept His Presence

The LORD turned to him and said, "Go in this might of yours, and you shall save Israel from the hand of the Midianites. Have I not sent you?"

~ Judges 6:14

Gideon's fears galloped away before God's comforting words, "Peace be with you; do not fear, you shall not die" (v. 23). Have you experienced God in this powerful way – where His presence destroys your fears, frustrations, and excuses? With such presence comes invitation. What invitation do you hear? Your answer?

Lord of peace, I feel fearful and weak when I think about standing in Your presence. Then You come. You speak. Love flows from You to me. Fears fly away. In their place comes the absolute conviction: He has invited me into His work. I accept. Amen.

March 20

God Speaks and Tests Your Faith

*He brought the people down to the water. And the LORD said
to Gideon, "Everyone who laps from the water with
his tongue, as a dog laps, you shall set apart by himself;
likewise everyone who gets down on his knees to drink."*

~ Judges 7:5

Gideon found God's ways strange. Test an army by
the way they drink water. Fight armed with torches
and trumpets. Surprise! God's ways worked. They
will work for you, too. Have you learned them?
Have you tried them?

*God, I must say it. Your ways are strange. I do not
understand them. You just do not work the way we
humans do. Give me the faith to hear You speak,
understand, and follow Your ways. Amen.*

March 21

God's Ways or My Ways?

*Then the men of Israel said to Gideon, "Rule over us,
both you and your son, and your grandson also; for you
have delivered us from the hand of Midian."*

~ Judges 8:22

Gideon must have really struggled with his crises. First, he had to send 31,700 soldiers home and keep only 300. Then, after his victory, he had to send the people home without the king they wanted.

Yet Gideon's love relationship with God was so firm that he followed God's ways even when human ways were far more attractive. What human glory do you surrender to do it God's way?

I surrender all. No longer is my mind set on power over people and things. No longer will I strive for positions to make me important. I know the way of the servant. I will follow You. Amen.

March 22

Do it God's Way

They put away the foreign gods from among
them and served the Lord. *And His soul could*
no longer endure the misery of Israel.

~ Judges 10:16

God is interested in absolute surrender. He keeps working until you let Him be Lord of all. After taking every detour they could find, Israel finally turned back to God.

But they had to change. Those things they had most adored they destroyed. Are you willing to destroy what stands between you and a love relationship with God?

One true God, I seem to have tried all the other gods:
wealth, fame, family, fun, activity, self-pity, religion,
helping others. None of those satisfy me.
I cling to You and to You alone. Amen.

March 23

Obey and Experience God Even in Death

Samson called to the LORD, saying, "O Lord GOD, remember me, I pray! Strengthen me, I pray, just this once, O God, that I may with one blow take vengeance on the Philistines for my two eyes!"

~ Judges 16:28

Great potential totally wasted. That defined Samson's life. Then he faced death, one great moment of truth. He chose to die doing things God's way and experienced his greatest victory. Must you wait till death faces you to obey and experience God?

Giver of eternal life, I want my life to count now. I refuse to wait until death makes me face the ultimate moment of truth. I choose now to obey You. As I do, joy floods my soul, for in the obeying I find the experiencing. Amen.

March 24

God Supplies Your Needs

*Then she arose with her daughters-in-law that
she might return from the country of Moab, for she
had heard in the country of Moab that the Lord had
visited His people by giving them bread.*

~ Ruth 1:6

To be a servant of God, find out where the Master is, then go there. Naomi had trouble following this principle. She kept settling down, and God kept working somewhere else: Judah, Moab, and then Judah again. Most important in her many moves stood one reality. She saw God at work. Do you?

*O, Master on the move, I want to sit down and
stay here for a while. Don't You ever call time out?
But at least, Lord, I see You at work. As long
as You work, I will work, too. Amen.*

March 25

Creating Human Love

Then Naomi said to her daughter-in-law, "Blessed be he of the LORD, who has not forsaken His kindness to the living and the dead! This man is a relation of ours, one of our close relatives."

~ Ruth 2:20

Ruth desperately worked to get food to eat. Suddenly, she found God had worked through her for an even greater purpose: creating human love that would produce Israel's greatest king.

God is always kind because He is always pursuing a love relationship with You. What are you pursuing? Do you turn to God only in moments of need?

Supplier of all my needs, You understand every part and every minute of my life. You provide for needs before I realize I have them. I give all of my life to You. Amen.

March 26

God Invites You
to Sacrificial Love

*Then Naomi her mother-in-law said to her, "My daughter,
shall I not seek security for you, that it may be well with you?"*
~ Ruth 3:1

If you have an obedience problem, you have a love
problem. Ruth had no obedience problem. She
risked her reputation and livelihood because she
obeyed the voice of God that spoke through her
mother-in-law. God rewarded her risk. What have
you risked because you love God?

*Sacrificial Lamb, I must sacrifice reputation,
comfort, job, and family to obey You. That is hard for
me. Help me lay aside pride and desire for comfort
so I may obey Your invitation. Amen.*

March 27

God Speaks
Through His People

Stay this night, and in the morning it shall be that if he will perform the duty of a close relative for you – good; let him do it. But if he does not want to perform the duty for you, then I will perform the duty for you, as the LORD lives! Lie down until morning.

~ Ruth 3:13

Boaz and Ruth faced a most difficult circumstance. They wanted to marry but custom said someone else had prior claim on Ruth. They let the normal course of circumstances work out, knowing God would reveal His purposes. Do you have faith to look at life's circumstances from God's viewpoint, not your own?

Lord, You can work Your will in every circumstance I face. Give me the eye of faith and the heart of patience to see and wait for You. Amen.

March 28

Who Is My Family?

Naomi said, "Turn back, my daughters; why
will you go with me? Are there still sons in
my womb, that they may be your husbands?"

~ Ruth 1:11

Ruth faced a hopeless situation. Husband dead, along with her father-in-law. Poverty faced her in Moab. Racial prejudice faced her in Judah. Even mother Naomi could offer no hope.

Still, the inner voice said, "Go with Naomi." She went. Have you described your crisis of belief to God? Do you have faith to go even when the prospects look dim and dark?

My Light in life's darkness, I am lonely. No one claims
me anymore. I have to choose to go somewhere and do
something, but no choice is inviting. Show me Your
way, and I will follow, even into the darkness. Amen.

March 29

Expand Your Family

Boaz took Ruth and she became his wife; and when he went in to her, the LORD gave her conception, and she bore a son.

~ Ruth 4:13

We say that God can interrupt us anytime He wants. We just don't expect Him to do it. Ruth never expected God to interrupt her the way He did; new home, new work, new husband, new baby.

Wonderful additions to her family, but certainly calls for life adjustments. Are you truly ready to say, Lord, interrupt me any way You want?

Interrupter of routine, prepare me for new relationships, new work, new hope, I want escape from the dullness of routine, but I crave its security. Let me find security in You. Interrupt my life. Amen.

March 30

Eternal Benefits of Obedience

Boaz begot Obed; Obed begot Jesse, and Jesse begot David.
~ Ruth 4:21-22

The benefits of obedience are beyond our imagination. Boaz and Ruth became parents, grandparents, and great-grandparents.

This gave the world King David, Israel's greatest hero until Jesus, who was also their descendant.

The benefits of obedience to a needy, widowed foreigner will be known only in eternity. Do you look forward to eternal benefits of obedience?

Life's benefits come only from You. Yet I still grab for temporal benefits that fly through my hands into the dim unknown. Today I place my hand in Yours and walk obediently down life's way with You. Amen.

April

The LORD is my strength and my shield;
my heart trusted in Him, and I am helped. ~ Psalm 28:7

God Establishes His Authoritative Word

So Elkanah her husband said to her, "Do what seems best to you; wait until you have weaned him. Only let the LORD establish His word." Then the woman stayed and nursed her son until she had weaned him.

~ 1 Samuel 1:23

Hannah's relationship with God led her to change lifelong habits. God had begun a work in her life and she dedicated herself to ensure that God's promise would be fulfilled.

How determined are you to see God's work accomplished? How is this affecting your habits?

God, You are at work in my life. What an amazing statement. Keep the amazement alive so my life is transformed, my habits changed, and my life dominated by You. Amen.

April 1

God's Love Relationship Changes Your Heart

*So it was, when he had turned his back to go
from Samuel, that God gave him another heart;
and all those signs came to pass that day.*

~ 1 Samuel 10:9

God allows no competitors in a love relationship. Saul had a marvelous chance to learn this lesson. God pursued Saul in love, performing miraculous signs and even giving Saul a fresh start.

But Saul refused to learn. Look back at all God has done to pursue a love relationship with you. Who is competition for Him in your life?

*Center of my life, vanquish all competition for
Your love. Turn my efforts to pursuing a relationship
with You. Help me see the miraculous works You
are performing in my life. Amen.*

April 2

God Invites You to Obey Him Completely

"Now go and attack Amalek, and utterly destroy all that they have, and do not spare them. But kill both man and woman, infant and nursing child, ox and sheep, camel and donkey."

~ 1 Samuel 15:3

God called Saul to be an agent of discipline, punishing the wicked Amalekites. Saul and his followers decided they knew how much discipline to inflict. God gave no commendation for a job half-done. He expected total obedience. Are you like Saul, wanting to only obey God halfway?

All-just God, forgive me when I play God with Your orders. It is so natural to hear what You command and then pat myself on the back when I do the part I like. Help me obey absolutely. Amen.

April 3

God Speaks to
Reveal His Ways

*"I greatly regret that I have set up Saul as king, for
he has turned back from following Me, and has not
performed My commandments." And it grieved
Samuel, and he cried out to the LORD all night.*

~ 1 Samuel 15:11

Never determine the truth of a situation by looking
at the circumstances. Samuel disliked God's message but cried out in prayer all night until he was
sure he had God's Word.

Then, even with personal regret, he acted obediently. Do you let circumstances change the way you
respond to God's Word? Or do you keep on praying
until you understand?

*Loving Father, I do not understand. Sometimes
the word You speak to me is just not what I want
to hear. I will keep wrestling with You.
Show me clearly Your holy ways. Amen.*

April 4

Can God Win the Victory?

*If he is able to fight with me and kill me, then we will
be your servants. But if I prevail against him, then
you shall be our servants and serve us.*

~ *1 Samuel 17:9*

David refused to rely on human wisdom for guidance. He asked for God's direction and he had to trust God. Goliath offered an awfully good reason not to trust God.

Neither Saul nor David's brothers offered help. Alone, he faced the crisis. God or Goliath? Which would you trust?

*Almighty, giants still pace the land. Financial bills,
work pressures, influence peddlers, sexual allures,
and broken relationships haunt me. Lift my eyes to the
heavens. Only there can I find true help, for Your fights
are always against giants, and You always win. Amen.*

April 5

Retreat to Win

*David said to Jonathan, "Indeed tomorrow is
the New Moon, and I should not fail to sit with the
king to eat. But let me go, that I may hide in the
field until the third day at evening."*

~ 1 Samuel 20:5

For David, his entire life had to be adjusted to God,
who anointed him king. But Saul called him to royal service and the great worship feast of the month
beckoned.

Family and boss expected him at worship. God
called him to the wilderness. How could he become
king there? Still, David followed. Are you willing to
endure the wilderness to follow God?

*Guide of all pilgrims, to achieve Your God-sized goals
will upset my secure nest. Push me out so that I find
security and direction from You and You alone. Amen.*

April 6

Wait for God's Time

*He said to his men, "The L*ORD *forbid that I should do this thing to my master, the L*ORD*'s anointed, to stretch out my hand against him, seeing he is the anointed of the L*ORD*."*

~ 1 Samuel 24:6

David knew he was to become king. Only one person, Saul, stood in the way. David had perfect opportunity. Kill Saul, and become king. That was the human way. That was not God's way.

David trusted God's promise and waited for God's time. Do you have patience to wait to achieve God's purpose in God's time?

Lord of all time, slow me down. Let me work Your work, but only in Your timing. I trust Your plan and Your ways. Amen.

God's at Work in Your Life

*There was a long war between the house of Saul
and the house of David. But David grew stronger
and stronger, and the house of Saul grew weaker.*

~ 2 Samuel 3:1

The Bible is designed to help you understand the ways of God. Often the Bible simply describes what we call history without mentioning God. The person in a love relationship with God knows how God acts and therefore sees God giving David strength and Saul weakness. Can you see God at work even when no one points a finger and says, "There He is working again"?

*Controller of my universe, be so close to me that
I know Your ways and recognize You at work –
even without miraculous signs. Let me be part
of the strong work You do. Amen.*

April 8

God Adopts You As His Own

"I will be His Father, and he shall be My son. If he commits iniquity, I will chasten him with the rod of men and with the blows of the sons of men. But My mercy shall not depart from him, as I took it from Saul, whom I removed from before you."

~ 2 Samuel 7:14-15

God takes you into a Father/child relationship, the closest relationship possible. He gives you perfect love, surrounding you with His mercy. David experienced God in this Father/child relationship. Have you?

My Father, You are not just someone far removed in the heavens. You are as close to me as anyone can possibly get. I take Your hand in mine and walk daily in love with You. Amen.

April 9

Act on God's Words

*King David sent to Zadok and Abiathar the priests, saying,
"Speak to the elders of Judah, saying, 'Why are you the last to
bring the king back to his house, since the words of all Israel
have come to the king, to his very house?'"*

~ 2 Samuel 19:11

Only God can give you the kind of specific directions you need to accomplish His purposes. David's religious leaders had to learn this lesson. They read the signs of the time. God spoke the real signs to them through David. Are you listening to see through whom God is speaking. Or are you trying to figure it out for sure on your own?

*God of the church, bring me so close to You that
I can hear the first words You say. Give me wisdom
to act as soon as I hear You. Amen.*

God Reveals His Purpose

There was a famine in the days of David for three years,
year after year; and David inquired of the LORD. And
the LORD answered, "It is because of Saul and his
bloodthirsty house, because he killed the Gibeonites."

~ 2 Samuel 21:1

To understand your bad or difficult circumstances, God's perspective is vital. Famine hurt David's people. He knew he had to find God's purpose in it.

God faithfully showed him what brought on divine discipline. In hard times, do you focus on circumstances or on God?

Times are so bad, God, that they distract me
from my relationship with You. Let me see
You above my circumstances. Amen.

April 11

Which Leader Must I Follow?

All the people were in a dispute throughout all the tribes of
Israel, saying, "The king saved us from the hand of our
enemies, he delivered us from the hand of the Philistines, and
now he has fled from the land because of Absalom."

~ 2 Samuel 19:9

Israel lost David's leadership. Confusion reigned. The people mistook a human leader for God, and therefore, saw themselves as powerless without David. Do you have faith to find God's way without a leader to show it to you?

Lord of Hosts, You alone are my leader. Forgive me
when I put a person in Your place and think that
I cannot know where to go without the person.
My faith is in You, not in a person. Amen.

April 12

Accept God's Discipline

*David arose from the ground, washed and
anointed himself, and changed his clothes; and he
went into the house of the LORD and worshiped.*

~ 2 Samuel 12:20

David knew life would go on after the death of his
son and after his horrible sin. The hard part was
how he would live: in remorse, mourning, and
defeat? Or in confident faith? What hard time has
tested your faith? How did you respond?

*Forgiving God, forgive my sin and my willingness
to wallow in defeat. Give me confident faith to
continue in spite of my shortcomings. Amen.*

April 13

Shout for Victory

*I have kept the ways of the L*ORD*,*
and have not wickedly departed from my God.

~ 2 Samuel 22:22

God is interested in developing your character but He will never let you go too far astray without discipline to bring you back.

That is the story of David's life: from sin with Bathsheba to a final acclamation that sin no longer dominated his life. Then he could shout joyfully for victory over sin. Have you kept God's ways? Then sing for victory!

God of the second chance, thank You for not giving up on me. I have endured Your discipline. You have brought me back to Yourself. Now I shout for victory over sin and pledge anew to walk in Your ways. Amen.

A God-Sized Task

*Now the LORD my God has given me rest on every
side; there is neither adversary nor evil occurrence.*

~ 1 Kings 5:4

The moment you know that God is doing something
where you are, your life will be thrown in contrast
to God. Solomon saw God at work clearly. He responded immediately, setting to work to build a
house for God. What clear work of God do you see?
What does that call you to do?

*One whose work never ceases, reveal Your work to me. In
my church, in my family, in our state, across the world,
make me aware of the mighty things You are doing.
Wherever You send, I will go on a God-sized task. Amen.*

Forgiveness for Sin

Forgive Your people who have sinned against You, and all their transgressions which they have transgressed against You; and grant them compassion before those who took them captive, that they may have compassion on them.

~ 1 Kings 8:50

Because we are in a love relationship with God, He forgives us when we ask. Forgiveness binds us close to Him, for we depend on His mercy and love. Confess your sin. Thank God for forgiving and loving You.

Compassionate One, I have experienced You in the mystery of forgiveness. Thank You that You love sinners. I do love You because You are You. Amen.

April 16

God Invites You
to a New Assignment

He said to Jeroboam, "Take for yourself ten pieces, for thus says the LORD, the God of Israel: 'Behold, I will tear the kingdom out of the hand of Solomon and will give ten tribes to you.'"

~ 1 Kings 11:31

Knowing God only comes through experience as He reveals Himself to you. Such revelation often comes in an invitation to a new assignment. God's prophet handed the invitation to Jeroboam: Be king of part of My people. What invitation has revealed God in a personal way to You?

God, in worship You became personal to me.
I met You. You had a hand outstretched inviting
me to Your work. Here I am, ready to go off on my
new assignment. Thanks, Lord. Amen.

April 17

A Call to Inaction

Thus says the LORD: "You shall not go up nor fight against your brethren the children of Israel. Let every man return to his house, for this thing is from Me."

~ 1 Kings 12:24

Judah wanted to see God in action. They wanted to experience Him as a Divine Warrior. Instead, He sent them home. Still, they encountered Him in the call to inaction. Have you heard God say, "Be still and know I am God"?

You are the Divine One. My faith does not depend on being where the action is. As long as You show me what You want, I will be content with the experience of You. Amen.

Obey the Ridiculous

If these people go up to offer sacrifices in the house of the
LORD at Jerusalem, then the heart of this people will turn
back to their lord, Rehoboam king of Judah, and they will
kill me and go back to Rehoboam king of Judah.

~ 1 Kings 12:27

Jeroboam saw clearly that Israel needed its own
worship place to prevent the people from giving
loyalty elsewhere.

God never gave a command to Jeroboam to build
a temple, but he built two. His disobedience spelled
doom for Israel. What obvious thing do you want to
do even though God has said nothing?

God who speaks, I think I know what is
necessary for Your kingdom. But You remain
silent. Okay, Lord, I give up. I will wait
even though it seems ridiculous. Amen.

April 19

Dare to Risk

Obadiah went to meet Ahab, and
told him; and Ahab went to meet Elijah.

~ 1 Kings 18:16

Obadiah faced an impossible task. Loyal to God, he worked for King Ahab. Ahab wanted to find Elijah, the prophet. Suddenly, Elijah appeared to Obadiah, saying, "Tell the king Elijah is here." But Obadiah knew the prophet's habit of disappearing. Dare he report to the king? Obadiah took the risk. Dare you speak up and tell the church the God-sized task He has presented you?

You dare us to risk all for You. We cannot do it.
But You can. Give me faith. I will join You in doing
the impossible, even at the risk of my life. Amen.

April 20

Risking Everything to Obey

*Naboth said to Ahab, "The L*ORD *forbid that I*
should give the inheritance of my fathers to you!"

~ *1 Kings 21:3*

Naboth knew God's will: Israel must protect the
property rights of each clan for it was God's property. But the king demanded the land, and had a fine
financial package for Naboth.

Two choices: Take the package, or die. Naboth
chose death. What situation do you know is absolutely wrong yet socially or financially essential?
What is your decision?

God, what can I do? I want to follow You,
but I need the money. Help me, Lord. I will obey.
I will experience You, even if that means experiencing
You in death and resurrection. Amen.

God Anoints His Leaders

Then he took the mantle of Elijah that had fallen from him,
and struck the water, and said, "Where is the LORD God of
Elijah?" And when he also had struck the water, it was
divided this way and that; and Elisha crossed over.

~ 2 Kings 2:14

When you come to God as His servant, He first molds and shapes you into His instrument. God used Elijah to mold and shape Elisha. Then God took Elijah away and worked through him, not Elisha, to accomplish His purpose. Do you trust that He is preparing you for the work He has planned all along?

Shaper of my life, bring me to maturity and give me the
equipment I need to accomplish Your work. I will do
Your work when You please. Amen.

God Is Faithful to His Promises

*Yet the L*ORD *would not destroy Judah, for the sake*
of His servant David, as He promised him to give
a lamp to him and his sons forever.

~ 2 Kings 8:19

History looked bleak for God's people. Doom time
had come. God had surely had enough, but God's
word surprised them. He refused to give up on His
people. Why? Because He is faithful by nature.

   He does what He promises. Are you expecting
God to end this evil world soon? Check with God
again. Has He fulfilled His promises?

Righteous heavenly Father, I live in an evil age and
I really expect You to bring final judgment upon us.
We deserve it. But I will trust You to decide how to
rule this world. I will do what You say. Amen.

April 23

God Invites You to
Start the Discipline

"You shall strike down the house of Ahab your master, that I may avenge the blood of My servants the prophets, and the blood of all the servants of the LORD, at the hand of Jezebel."

~ 2 Kings 9:7

How can God invite a person to start such a blood bath? Is that love? Normally, we would say, "No way!" Then we look to God in faith. What do you see? An angry selfish tyrant invigorated by enemy blood? Or a sad Father forced to punish disobedience and sin? Are you willing to take the tough tasks for God, or may He invite you to do only the glory tasks?

Holy God, we sinners force You to discipline and judge us. Forgive me, Father, for being part of the world's sin. Use me as Your instrument, no matter what the task may be. Amen.

God Speaks to
Announce His Plan

*The LORD said to Jehu, "Because you have done well in
doing what is right in My sight, and have done to the
house of Ahab all that was in My heart, your sons shall
sit on the throne of Israel to the fourth generation."*

~ 2 Kings 10:30

When God spoke, the person knew what God said.
Jehu knew God's word of blessing and promise. He
was certain God had spoken directly to him. Do
you have this certainty? Are you sure of what God
is saying today?

One who chooses to speak to Your people,
I come listening. I put everything out of my life
that would prevent me from hearing You. I listen
for Your voice. Speak, Lord. Amen.

April 25

Whom Do You Trust?

You speak of having plans and power for war; but they are mere
words. And in whom do you trust, that you rebel against me?

~ 2 Kings 18:20

Faith is believing that the God who called us to the assignments is the One who will provide for their accomplishment. Hezekiah faced a tremendous crisis. The strongest army in the world threatened his city.

But God had the plan. Trust and wait for the God who made him king to make him free. Who would you trust? The world's most powerful army, or a word of promise?

Lord of Hosts, I must have a God-sized escape
from the situation I am in. The enemy surrounds me.
What can I do? I throw myself in faith on You.
You have delivered me. Do it again, Lord. Amen.

Hope in the Presence of Death

*Then she called to her husband, and said, "Please send
me one of the young men and one of the donkeys,
that I may run to the man of God and come back."*

~ 2 Kings 4:22

Elisha had to leave family and career, burn his farm equipment, and kill his oxen. When he made these adjustments, he was in a position to obey God.

As a result, he was ready to help his dear friend when she lost her son. He shared God's love with her, and God used him to restore her son. How do losses you have suffered affect your love relationship with God?

*Father of the Crucified One, You understand
my loss. You know the deep hurt I feel. I bring it
all to You. Teach me Your ways through what is lost.
I trust and follow You. Amen.*

April 27

Absolute Trust

He trusted in the LORD God of Israel, so that
after him was none like him among all the
kings of Judah, nor who were before him.

~ 2 Kings 18:5

If you are obedient, God will work some wonderful things through you. But be very careful, because pride may prevent you from giving God the glory. God scared off the entire Assyrian army for Hezekiah. Sadly, God also had to punish a proud Hezekiah who showed off His God-given wealth to the Babylonians.

How are you responding as you obey and God begins to work through you? Can you meet pride's challenge?

All-merciful God, You are wonderful. You have
given me an obedient heart. Now protect me from
pride that would lead me away from You. Amen.

God's Work Is More Powerful Than Human Armies

The inhabitants of Jebus said to David, "You shall not come in here!" Nevertheless David took the stronghold of Zion (that is, the City of David).

~ 1 Chronicles 11:5

Anyone who will take the time to enter into an intimate relationship with God can see Him do extraordinary things.

David, the shepherd boy, became king and faced a professional army considered invincible. A God-sized task? Certainly. One God accomplished? Surely. What task has you stymied? Can He accomplish it through you even though it is impossible for you?

Mighty One, You pursued me and formed this wonderful love relationship with me, but now I see only a blank wall. Open my faith eyes to see You at work where I have given up. Amen.

April 29

God's Eternal Covenant

*He is the LORD our God; His judgments are in all the
earth. Remember His covenant forever, the word which
He commanded for a thousand generations.*

~ 1 Chronicles 16:14

A love relationship with God is more important
than any other factor in your life. That love relationship is a covenant, a treaty He made with you to
love you and be your God so that you could love
Him and be part of His kingdom. Is the Lord your
God? How much do you love Him?

*Lover of my soul, I love You with all my heart, all my
mind, all my soul, with all that You have created me to
be. Thank You that You are the God of covenant who
wants to be in love with me eternally. Amen.*

April 30

May

"Be still, and know that I am God." ~ *Psalm 46:10*

God Invites You
to Prepare for Worship

Let us bring the ark of our God back to us,
for we have not inquired at it since the days of Saul.

~ 1 Chronicles 13:3

When God is about to do something, He lets His servants know what He is about to do and invites them to join Him in His work. God was about to use David to establish Israel as a model for kingship and messianic promise. First, He invited the people to a renewal of worship. Does God want your worship practices to change before He begins a new work through you?

Our Praise and our Glory, we accept Your invitation
to worship. We come to sing Your praises,
to testify to the work You are doing among us,
to confess our sins, and to hear You speak. Amen.

May 1

God Speaks to
Direct Your Path

The children of the Levites bore the ark of God on their shoulders, by its poles, as Moses had commanded according to the word of the LORD.

~ 1 Chronicles 15:15

God's Word showed David how to begin a new stage in the history of Israel's worship. Only as he obeyed exactly, did God bless His efforts. Are you trying to follow something specific from God's Word? Do you want to put your own personal twist on the way you follow? Or will you do it God's way?

Author of the inspired Bible, speak through Your Word to me today. I want to know Your ways and Your purposes. I will not try to dilute or redirect them. I will follow in Your paths. Amen.

May 2

God or the Program?

As for you, my son Solomon, know the God of your father,
and serve Him with a loyal heart and with a willing mind;
*for the L*ORD *searches all hearts and understands*
all the intent of the thoughts.

~ 1 Chronicles 28:9

Solomon faced a crisis. Did he believe in divine destiny where God would fulfill the promise to David, or did He believe in God Himself in a personal love relationship? David encouraged Solomon to know God. Too often, Solomon knew only the desire for power. Do you know a program or a Person?

God of our fathers, only Your ways lead
to meaning. I want to know You in a personal
love relationship forever. Amen.

Forsake the Family

These were the men who came to David at Ziklag
while he was still a fugitive from Saul the son of Kish;
and they were among the mighty men, helpers in the war.
They were of Benjamin, Saul's brethren.

~ 1 Chronicles 12:1-2

Saul's soldiers were connected to Saul professionally and through bloodlines. Yet circumstances clearly revealed God working through David. These courageous soldiers left Saul and went to David. They forsook friends and family for the truth of God. Has God's invitation convinced you that a major adjustment is in order?

Changer of my life, why do You want to make so
many adjustments in my life? But I will do it Your way.
What is the first step I need to take? Amen.

A Life of Obedience

*He died in a good old age, full of days and riches
and honor; and Solomon his son reigned in his place.*

~ 1 Chronicles 29:28

The story of David features sin in many chapters: Bathsheba, Adonijah, Absalom. Still, at the end God praised him and honored him as a person who obeyed and experienced Him.

Focus on your life of obedience. Will you continue to obey until God calls you to a new realm of experience with Him?

*Giver of life and death, I thank You that You have
pursued a love relationship with me all these years.
I pledge anew my remaining days to serve and obey You,
no matter the adjustments You call on me to make. Amen.*

God Prepares the Way

Hiram also said: Blessed be the LORD God of Israel, who made heaven and earth, for He has given King David a wise son, endowed with prudence and understanding, who will build a temple for the LORD and a royal house for himself!

~ 2 Chronicles 2:12

With God's help, Solomon became very successful by the world's standards. God prepared the way for Him to succeed, but Solomon began measuring everything in worldly standards, not God's. What standards do you use to measure success in your life?

Judge of all, I tend to be proud of what I have accomplished. Only when I join in Your work are my accomplishments wonderful. Amen.

God's Love Relationship
Fulfills His Purposes

Blessed be the LORD your God, who delighted in you, setting you on His throne to be king for the LORD your God! Because your God has loved Israel, to establish them forever, therefore He made you king over them, to do justice and righteousness.

~ 2 Chronicles 9:8

Solomon had the nation's highest position. How? Because God loved him. Because God wanted to show all nations His righteousness and justice. Where would you be without God's love?

Source of all righteousness, You have led me to where I am now. Show me the opportunities You have available so I can fulfill Your purposes. Amen.

May 7

God Invites You to
See His Salvation

You will not need to fight in this battle. Position yourselves,
stand still and see the salvation of the LORD,
who is with you, O Judah and Jerusalem!

~ 2 Chronicles 20:17

King Jehoshaphat's job was to protect his people from their enemies. God took over this job and pushed Jehoshaphat to the sidelines to watch God at work.

Are you in God's way, trying to do something He wants to do? Will you step to the sidelines and let God work?

Savior, too often I depend upon my own skills to
get the job done and get through the trouble.
Help me this time to hear Your voice and do
things Your way. Let me see Your salvation. Amen.

Judgment Is Real

*Behold, the L*ORD *will strike your people with a*
serious affliction – your children, your wives,
and all your possessions.

~ 2 Chronicles 21:14

In the Old Testament God spoke in many different
ways. He had Elijah send a letter to King Jehoram, a
letter dealing with very practical matters: the physi-
cal health of Jehoram's family. Have you talked to
God about the health of your family? What means
has He used to give you an answer?

Informer of Your people about Your ways, self, and
purposes, I face temptations and crises in my own
family life. I need to know how You are at work in this
situation. Show me, I pray, and I will obey. Amen.

May 9

Whose Advice Is True?

Do not be stiff-necked, as your fathers were, but yield
yourselves to the LORD; and enter His sanctuary, which
He has sanctified forever, and serve the LORD your God,
that the fierceness of His wrath may turn away from you.

~ 2 Chronicles 30:8

People in the north were in captivity to a foreign
king. Suddenly, word came from the south. "Come
back and join us in worshiping God in Jerusalem."

But how would the foreign king react? Do you
have voices calling you in two directions? Which
will you obey?

God of anger and judgment, so many people give advice
that I do not know which direction to turn. Give me
faith to walk in Your way and in no other. Amen.

May 10

Age Makes No Difference

They broke down the altars of the Baals in his presence, and
the incense altars which were above them he cut down; and the
wooden images, the carved images, and the molded images he
broke in pieces, and made dust of them and scattered it on the
graves of those who had sacrificed to them.

~ 2 Chronicles 34:4

Josiah became king at age eight, reformer of the
nation's religion at sixteen, repairer of the temple
at twenty-six. At that time, he discovered God's lost
Word and made it the law of the land. When are you
going to start showing the world what God can do
through one yielded life?

Ageless Lord, when You free me from
sin's dominion and point me on the road
to obedience, no one can imagine what You can
do through me. Do it, Lord. Start today. Amen.

May 11

God Hears You

"Because your heart was tender ... and you humbled yourself
before Me, and you tore your clothes and wept before Me,
I also have heard you," says the LORD.

~ *2 Chronicles 34:27*

When God hears you, you experience Him. Experiencing Him comes only when you obey Him. What a wonderful circle to be in: obey, experience, be heard, obey, experience. Are you in the "God hears you" circle of experience? Exclaim your joy to God!

Thank You that You listen to me. Most of the
time all I need is for You to listen. Then I can
go out in obedience, experiencing You and seeing
You work through me. Amen.

Get Started!

On the first day of the first month he began his journey from
Babylon, and on the first day of the fifth month he came to
Jerusalem, according to the good hand of his God upon him.
~ Ezra 7:9

God gave Ezra a God-sized task: Take people across
the desert from Babylon to Jerusalem. Ezra got
authority from the Persian government and financial resources.

He could have been proud of his political skill.
Instead, Ezra pointed to the Source of all he accomplished. Are you sitting pretty with resources and
authority? To whom do you give credit?

Faithful Pursuer of my soul, with all the activities
I am engaged in and the decisions I have to make,
I know that most important is Your work to renew
Your people. Use me to get things started. Amen.

God's Love Relationship
with Sinful, Broken People

For we were slaves. Yet our God did not forsake us in our bondage; but He extended mercy to us in the sight of the kings of Persia, to revive us, to repair the house of our God, to rebuild its ruins, and to give us a wall in Judah and Jerusalem.

~ *Ezra 9:9*

Most of Israel had no social standing. They were exiled slaves in a foreign land, or in their own land serving foreign rulers. God forgot no one and gave love to all. How has God shown His love in your situation? How have you shown your love to Him?

You remember us forever. We cannot move too far away, get too deep in debt or become too insignificant in society. You still show mercy. Thank You, my Lord and my God. Amen.

May 14

Will You Accept God's Invitation?

Then I said to them, "You see the distress that we are in,
how Jerusalem lies waste, and its gates are burned with fire.
Come and let us build the wall of Jerusalem,
that we may no longer be a reproach."

~ Nehemiah 2:17

God's ways and thoughts are so different from yours and mine that they will often sound wrong or crazy. Almost 100 years after Israel first returned from exile in Babylon, Nehemiah found the city still in ruins.

God's way was obvious: Get to work. Human ways were equally obvious: Why bother after this long? Will you accept God's crazy invitation – no matter how others react?

Your ways are so different, God. Your invitation makes no sense to the people around me. But I will be a fool for You. Who knows? Maybe others will follow. Amen.

May 15

God's Written Word

*So they read distinctly from the book, in the Law
of God; and they gave the sense, and helped
them to understand the reading.*

~ Nehemiah 8:8

You will not obey God if you do not believe Him.
You cannot believe Him if you do not love Him. You
cannot love Him unless you know Him. Ezra and
Nehemiah reintroduced Israel to their God by reading and explaining His written word.

Do you want to obey, believe, love, and know
God so strongly that you devote an hour each day
to His Word?

*Inspirer of the holy Word, speak to me so
that I may know You and love You.
I will read Your Word and obey it. Amen.*

Act or Perish

All know that any man or woman who goes into the inner court to the king, who has not been called, he has but one law: put all to death, except the one to whom the king holds out the golden scepter, that he may live. Yet I myself have not been called to go in to the king these thirty days.

~ Esther 4:11

Esther faced a serious crisis of belief. Either she risked death by going before the king and revealing her faith or her nation would die. What is the most serious decision God has set before you? What risk are you willing to take for God?

God who acts in mighty ways, why am I so fearful to act in even small ways? Show me the risks I must take. I will take them. Amen.

May 17

Willing to Die

Go, gather all the Jews who are present in Shushan, and fast for me; neither eat nor drink for three days, night or day. My maids and I will fast likewise. And so I will go to the king, which is against the law; and if I perish, I perish!

~ Esther 4:16

Esther, the orphan, became queen of the empire. The day came when God said, "Time to adjust. Protect yourself or your people."

Esther chose to protect her people, even if it cost her life. Will spiritual awakening in our generation come from anything less than faith ready to die in God's work?

Father of renewal and revival, change our church, our city, our state, our nation, our world. Make Your presence so real that no one can ignore You. Amen.

May 18

A Humble Hero

Now all the acts of his power and his might,
and the account of the greatness of Mordecai,
to which the king advanced him, are they not written in
the book of the chronicles of the kings of Media and Persia?

~ Esther 10:2

Who would have selected Mordecai as the person
destined for greatness? Only one who knew his faith.
Does God have you destined for greatness? Only if
you, like Mordecai, humbly obey in whatever work
God has given you today. Obedience in small works
for God today prepares you for greater works tomorrow.

Always-working God, no one expects what You do.
I make no claim to fame nor do I expect earthly
honor or reward. I simply want to see
how to be an overcomer for You. Amen.

May 19

God Works in Mysterious Ways

The LORD said to Satan, "Behold,
he is in your hand, but spare his life."

~ Job 2:6

Once you know God's will, you can adjust your life to Him. The focus needs to be on God, not on your life. Job had a tough time understanding this, because both God and Satan were strongly focused on his life.

Job struggled to find God's will and finally found only God. Are you demanding that God answer questions He is not ready to answer?

Mysterious One, make me a part of
Your mysterious work, even when I do
not understand what is happening. Amen.

May 20

In Life's Darkest Moments

The LORD blessed the latter days of Job more than his beginning; for he had fourteen thousand sheep, six thousand camels, one thousand yoke of oxen, and one thousand female donkeys. He also had seven sons and three daughters.

~ *Job 42:12*

God showed His love by trusting Job to endure the most horrifying of circumstances and by showing His presence when all was said and done.

Have life's circumstances hidden God's love from you? Can you believe that in these most difficult times, God is showing how much He trusts you?

Trusting God, I see only the darkness all around. Take my eyes off the circumstances to see Your hand of love at work even through the darkest moments. Amen.

May 21

God Invites You to Answer Him

*Then the L*ORD *answered Job out of the whirlwind,*
and said: "Now prepare yourself like a man;
I will question you, and you shall answer Me."

~ Job 40:6-7

Job had to endure Satan at work and friends scolding him. Finally God came with penetrating questions, demanding answers Job could not provide. Even in unanswerable questions Job became ready to obey and thus experienced God. Is God asking you questions you cannot answer? Will you quit questioning and start believing?

Master of the question-and-answer game,
I will no longer throw my questions at You,
demanding an answer before I serve You. You have
done all that is necessary in Jesus Christ. I love You
even when I do not understand You. Amen.

May 22

When You Are Humbled

Shall the one who contends with the Almighty
correct Him? He who rebukes God, let him answer it.

~ Job 40:2

Job wanted an experience with God more than anything else. The seeming absence of God was his central concern. God refused to give in to Job's demands. Only when God had humbled him could God speak to him. Are you making so many demands on God, that He cannot get through to talk to you?

Almighty One, You never promised life would be fair. You did promise, however, that You would never forsake me. Come to me in the way You desire. Teach me obedience, and cause me to experience You anew. Amen.

Faith in the Silent One

Listen, please, and let me speak; You said, "I will question you and you shall answer Me." I have heard of You by the hearing of the ear, but now my eye sees You.

~ Job 42:4-5

Job depended on what others told him about God when what he needed was a personal experience with God. That came only when he obeyed rather than rebelled. Is your faith in God, or in what someone else told you about God?

Silent One, I want to know You personally. I do not want faith in a principle or proposition. I want faith in the One whom I experience in love and obedience. Amen.

Repent from Wrong Attitudes

Therefore, I abhor myself, and repent in dust and ashes.

~ Job 42:6

Job had self-esteem and the esteem of everyone around him, at least until suffering came. Then, others sneered at his fake religion, and he hated himself for his attitude toward God.

Job had to give up his demands on God and admit that he had placed himself on an equal plane with God. Are you so pious that you have people fooled, yet know that you do not have the right attitude to God?

All-knowing Father, I have accepted what others have said about my goodness and piety. I have the trappings of religion but no ongoing love relationship with You. Forgive me. Amen.

Are You Fulfilling God's Assignment for You?

The LORD restored Job's losses when he prayed for his friends. Indeed the LORD gave Job twice as much as he had before.

~ Job 42:10

If Job needed anything, he needed patience. He was ready to give God assignments. He gave his friends assignments. He thought obedience was in defending God.

Finally, God got his ear and gave him the assignment: Pray for your friends. Are you so busy in religious arguments that you miss the assignment He has for you?

Lord, I stand ready to do whatever You say. I have no right to tell You how to run the world. Forgive my impatience. You are working. What part is mine? Amen.

God Works to Bless and Save

Salvation belongs to the L{\small ORD}.
Your blessing is upon Your people.

~ Psalm 3:8

We usually want God to speak to us so He can give us a devotional thought to make us feel good. In the Scripture, God is not often seen coming and speaking to people just for conversation's sake.

He was always up to something that was bringing salvation and blessing to His people. Are you ready to be a part of that work of blessing and salvation?

Savior, make me as serious about Your work
of salvation as You are. Don't let me be satisfied
with a good spiritual pep talk that makes me feel
good for a few hours. What is my part in
bringing blessing and salvation? Amen.

God Is Your Shepherd

The LORD is my shepherd. I shall not want.

~ Psalm 23:1

David knew how much his sheep depended on him and he wanted to protect them. But in God's love relationship, David played a role reversal. No longer was he the loving, protecting shepherd. He became a helpless, foolish sheep, totally dependent on God's love. Are you willing to give up the position of power control in order to experience God's love?

Shepherd of my life, I keep running away
like a foolish sheep, risking my life when there is
no hope of return. You show how much You
love me by coming to my rescue time and time again.
Please always be my Shepherd. Amen.

The Lord Is Good!

Oh, taste and see that the LORD is good;
blessed is the man who trusts in Him!

~ Psalm 34:8

Most of all, God wants you to love Him, but you cannot love what you do not experience. God uses every kind of language imaginable to show how much He wants you to experience Him in an eternal love relationship. What kind of experience do you need to trust God and love Him?

Food for my life, that is what You are.
I am nothing without daily nourishment from You.
You invite me to taste. I will. Feed me,
Lord, from Yourself. That is all I need. Amen.

God Speaks in Judgment

Our God shall come, and shall not keep silent;
a fire shall devour before Him, and it shall be very
tempestuous all around Him. He shall call to the heavens
from above, and to the earth, that He may judge His people.

~ Psalm 50:3-4

When God was about to do something in the Bible, He spoke to reveal His purposes and plans so his servants could be involved and accomplish His purposes. One purpose of God is to judge evil. Are you prepared to face God's judgment of evil and unbelief?

Judge of the universe, You alone have the right to punish
evil, for You alone are righteous. I know You are
coming to judge the world. Forgive my sins.
Renew a right spirit within me. Amen.

May 30

Widen Your Vision

O God, You have cast us off; You have broken us down;
You have been displeased; oh, restore us again!

~ *Psalm 60:1*

If the assignment you sense from God is some-thing you know you can handle, it probably is not from God. Israel knew of no assignment they could handle. All they could do was ask to be restored to God's grace. What must God do to make you realize the small things you think you are doing for Him are not His assignments for you?

You are larger than life, God. You see things
and make plans far beyond the scope of my vision.
Widen my vision. If it takes judgment,
send judgment upon me until I am ready to
accept the God-sized tasks You are offering. Amen.

June

*Praise the L*ORD*! Oh, give thanks to the L*ORD*, for He is good! For His mercy endures forever.* ~ Psalm 106:1

Humble Yourself Before God

*As for me, my prayer is to You, O Lord, in the
acceptable time; O God, in the multitude of Your
mercy, hear me in the truth of Your salvation.*

~ *Psalm 69:13*

In the good times Israel began to take God's salvation for granted. Only desperate times shook them out of their self-confidence in their relationship with God. Finally, they learned to cry out for help, knowing help would come only when God chose.

Do you need to make God the master of your beliefs, or are you content to worship a god you think you can control?

*Ruler of the universe, I get so confident that I
know everything about You. Humble me. Come with
Your spiritual tool kit and readjust my life until I
can join again in Your great work. Amen.*

June 1

Hope, Knowledge and Obedience

That they may set their hope in God, and not forget the works of God, but keep His commandments.

~ *Psalm 78:7*

Israel continued to live in hope, waiting for God to act. They forgot to see what God was up to at the moment and to find what He wanted them to do right then. God called on them to obey. They called on God to deliver. So, they had reached a stalemate.

Are you at a stalemate in your relationship with God because He does not do what you expect? What is He waiting for you to do?

Patient One, I seem to trust You only when You do what I want. You are the Creator and Master of the universe. Show me what I must do to obey. Amen.

June 2

God Works Among
the Heavenly Powers

God stands in the congregation of the mighty;
He judges among the gods.

~ Psalm 82:1

God has a right to interrupt your life. He is Lord. Even the heavenly powers had to learn this lesson. The psalmist pictured God in the regularly-scheduled meeting of heaven's general assembly.

God startled the members by pronouncing judgment on those who showed partiality and favored injustice. What is His verdict when you stand before Him for judgment?

King of Heaven, You stand for right and justice.
I will join You in Your uncommon work of
showing love to those who seldom experience it
and of fighting for justice and mercy for those
who cannot defend themselves. Amen.

June 3

Enjoy God's Presence

For a day in Your courts is better than a thousand.
I would rather be a door keeper in the house of my
God than dwell in the tents of wickedness.

~ Psalm 84:10

Worship with God overjoyed the psalmist. Worship seemed to be the place to spend eternity. Why go anywhere else? The most menial work in the place where God is appears better than any other kind of work where God is not present. Do you enjoy God's presence?

God above all, accept my praise. A love relationship
with You means I get to spend all my time with You.
I want nothing else than to know I am in Your
presence. Show me where You are working now,
so I can go to work with You. Amen.

God Invites You to Praise

*Praise the L*ORD*! Praise, O servants of*
*the L*ORD*, praise the name of the L*ORD*!*

~ *Psalm 113:1*

To worship is to acknowledge God as worthy of your praise. Do you enjoy giving someone else credit for their accomplishments? Do you enjoy recommending someone else for a prize or position because they deserve it? Each of these activities is a part of worship, except the One to whom you give credit is God Himself. Do you need to practice paying Him compliments?

Chief Executive of the universe, I come simply to compliment You for You are marvelous, glorious, brilliant, wonderful, extraordinary. I will never find words sufficient to express how great You are. Thank You, God, for inviting me to praise Your name. Amen.

Encounter God in Scripture

Your word is a lamp to my feet and a light
to my path. I have sworn and confirmed that
I will keep Your righteous judgments.

~ Psalm 119:105-106

Understanding spiritual truth does not lead you to an encounter with God, it is the encounter with God. If God has revealed spiritual truth to you through this passage of Scripture, you have encountered God Himself working in you! What do you reply to God as you encounter Him through His word?

Revealer of all truth, I come to Your Word seeking to know You. Continue to speak to me and let me encounter You, for only then do I truly live in a love relationship with You. Amen.

Separated from Home

By the rivers of Babylon, there we sat down,
yea, we wept when we remembered Zion.

~ Psalm 137:1

When the Israelites were exiles in Babylon, there was no place and seemingly no reason to worship. All they could do was cry and express their grief and anger. They did not seek a mission from God but cried to Him in hatred for vengeance on their enemies. Has your crisis of belief made you too desperate to have faith?

Now God, what is wrong? Nothing is going
right. Everything has taken a wrong turn. I know
I am supposed to worship and praise, but I see
nothing to worship about. I am too mad to worship.
Help me God. I want to worship. I want to love
You. Show me how to in this situation. Amen.

June 7

Praising Under
Divine Examination

Search me, O God, and know my heart; try me, and
know my anxieties; and see if there is any wicked way
in me, and lead me in the way everlasting.

~ Psalm 139:23-24

Any adjustment God expects you to make is for your own good. Even surrounded by wickedness, the psalmist asked God to look deep inside and reveal any adjustments that needed to be made.

Are you willing to take your eyes off your troubles long enough to ask God to show you the "wicked way" that lurks in your heart?

Searcher of my soul, find the deepest part of me
that I have hidden even from myself. Reveal any
wrong or hurtful thought. Distract me from my
troubles with Your revealing love. Amen.

June 8

Joy in God's Presence

Let Israel rejoice in their Maker; let the children of Zion be
joyful in their King. Let them praise His name with the dance;
let them sing praises to Him with the timbrel and harp.

~ Psalm 149:2-3

Obedience means joy and an uninterrupted fellowship with God. This joy bursts out in various ways
as we express our love and praise to God. Does joy
so flood your life that you call people to worship
God with you to express the exuberance of your
joy?

My King, I express my great love to You. I call on all
people I know to join me in singing and shouting and
praying and praising. We love You and want to tell the
world how wonderful it is to experience God. Amen.

God Works in Wisdom

The LORD by wisdom founded the earth; by understanding He established the heavens.

~ *Proverbs 3:19*

One look at creation shows God is at work. Only divine wisdom could plan and establish the wonderful world we live in, with its symmetry, beauty, and ability to sustain so many kinds of life. Do not ask if God is working. Instead, ask, "Where is God working so I can join in?" Do you want to find God at work?

Eternal One, You created time itself. You know the best use of every second I live. You have work I can do that will give purpose to my life and further Your kingdom. Yes, Lord, I want to work the work You created me to accomplish. Amen.

June 10

God Loves Like No Other

I love those who love me, and those
who seek me diligently will find me.

~ *Proverbs 8:17*

Proverbs pictures God's wisdom as a woman walking the streets calling you to follow her and know the
love that only God can give. Is there a love-shaped
hole in your heart? Only God can fill it. Only He can
create a true love relationship with You. He wants
to. Do you?

In Your wisdom You have chosen to love me even when
I am at my most unloveliest. You woo me and court me.
Why do I hide and seek a better offer? No one will love
me the way You do. I surrender to Your love. Amen.

God Leads You Away
From Immorality

Whoever is simple, let him turn in here! As for him who lacks understanding, she says to him, "Come, eat of my bread and drink of the wine I have mixed. Forsake foolishness and live, and go in the way of understanding."

~ Proverbs 9:4-6

Does your daily life flirt with immoral people and immoral actions? Do you have a love relationship with the world, or with God? God invites you to Himself. Such an invitation means to be holy as He is holy. Will you accept this invitation?

All-wise God, You are pure and holy. You lovingly invite me to live in the paths of Your wisdom. I will accept Your invitation to live pure and trust You to be right. Amen.

God Speaks
About His Word

He who despises the word will be destroyed, but
he who fears the commandment will be rewarded.

~ Proverbs 13:13

Once God has spoken to you through His Word, how you respond is crucial. You must adjust your life to the truth. How you respond shows how you really regard God's Word. Do you despise the Word? Or do you fear and follow the Word? Your daily life reveals the answer.

God of revelation, You have chosen to speak to us.
You do not dwell in silence. Thank You for the Word,
which is constantly before us to reveal You, Your ways,
and Your purposes. Give me faith and courage to
adjust my life to Your truth. Amen.

Walk in Truth

*Getting treasures by a lying tongue is the
fleeting fantasy of those who seek death.*

~ Proverbs 21:6

Obedience indicates faith in God. The world offers
you a different kind of faith – faith in your powers
to deceive others and to deceive God. God tells
you the truth: lying leads to dying, eternally. So the
choice is yours; believe God or believe your power
to deceive.

*Truth You are and truth You expect from me.
But I lie so well. No one knows I am not telling the
truth, and I can get what I want. But Your Word
challenges me to see the final consequences of my lies.
Forgive me, God. I will quit my lying right now. I will
trust in the Truth and ask You to give me life. Amen.*

June 14

Reject Pride

*If you have been foolish in exalting yourself, or if you
have devised evil, put your hand on your mouth.*

~ *Proverbs 30:32*

Life adjustment to God requires that you move from
working for God under your own abilities to being
totally dependent on God and His resources. Have
you made this adjustment? Or do you still place "I"
at the center of life? Can you learn to put your hand
on your mouth and stop exalting yourself?

*God, You keep pounding home the lesson. You know
what is right. You have the power to accomplish good
things. Your plans are best for me. Why does "I" keep
getting in my way so much? Shut me up. Teach me to
wait on You and listen to Your guidance. Amen.*

Help and Be Helped

She extends her hand to the poor, yes,
she reaches out her hands to the needy.

~ Proverbs 31:20

A basic assignment God gives His people through His Word is to take care of those who cannot care for themselves. Only when you begin to obey these basic assignments can you expect God to give You bigger tasks in His work. Are you still in the remedial courses of God's work, or are you ready to accept other assignments too?

Friend of the helpless, You constantly teach me
that I have resources only because You give
them to me for Your work. Forgive my selfishness.
Forgive my blindness to the needs of other people.
I will start Your basic work today. Amen.

June 16

A Burdensome Course

I set my heart to seek and search out by wisdom concerning all that is done under heaven; this burdensome task God has given to the sons of man, by which they may be exercised.

~ *Ecclesiastes 1:13*

As Solomon discovered, not every task God gives is exciting and glorious. Some tasks are burdensome and hard. They require all your energy and still do not seem to provide the rewards you expect. Are you willing to join God in the hard work too?

All-powerful God, Your ways are right, but they are not always fun. So often I join in the work and it appears to be hard and unrewarding. God, make the love relationship so real that I am willing to continue, even when the results are not what I want. Amen.

June 17

God's Love Relationship Brings Human Love

How fair is your love, my sister, my spouse!
How much better than wine is your love, and
the scent of your perfumes than all spices!

~ Song of Songs 4:10

From the Garden of Eden onwards, God has shown us that loneliness is not part of His ways for us. He leads us to a love relationship with Him that teaches us how to have a special love relationship with a mate. Are you letting God create the love qualities in you that make you a good mate for someone else?

God, You know my situation, You know how I ache for love and companionship. Bring love into my life. Teach me to love You so intimately that I can love a mate with Your kind of love. Amen.

June 18

God Invites You
to Accept His Joy

Go, eat your bread with joy, and drink your wine with
a merry heart; for God has already accepted your works.

~ Ecclesiastes 9:7

Solomon expected too much out of life and found
so much of it to be totally vain. God reminded him
to enjoy the simple things of life and quit trying to
earn His favor. God wants you to have joy. Do you
worry so much about life's unfairness that you lose
the joy God placed here for you? Accept His joy.

Joyous One who revels in life and all its possibilities,
lead me into quiet paths of simple joy while I wait to
find the larger work You have for me. Amen.

God Speaks through Proverbial Wisdom

Moreover, because the Preacher was wise, he still taught the people knowledge; yes, he pondered and sought out and set in order many proverbs.

~ Ecclesiastes 12:9

God spoke to Solomon through proverbs, that the people of his nation had collected over many centuries. Solomon then put these in order as part of God's written Word. Are you willing to ponder the wisdom God has given the people of your church and test it to see if God is speaking to you through the church?

Wise One of the ages, reveal Your wisdom to me. Open my heart and mind to see and hear You speaking in the many ways You choose. Amen.

June 20

Accept Life's Mysteries

Who knows what is good for man in life, all the days of
his vain life which he passes like a shadow? Who can
tell a man what will happen after him under the sun?

~ *Ecclesiastes 6:12*

Ecclesiastes always comes to the same conclusion:
Life is a mystery I cannot understand because I do
not have enough knowledge. That makes life seem
meaningless. Have you come to the same conclusion? Is it because you keep wanting to find meaning
in what you decide to do rather than finding what
God is doing?

Mysterious One, I constantly stand in a crisis of belief
because I want to predict what is good for me and what
my future holds. Father, You know I need to focus on
You and let You take care of my future. Help me to do
that. I will accept the mystery because I love You. Amen.

June 21

Act in the Face of Death

Whatever your hand finds to do, do it with your might;
for there is no work or device or knowledge or wisdom
in the grave where you are going.

~ Ecclesiastes 9:10

The day is coming when you will no longer be able to do anything. Are you letting fear of death or failure or wrong decisions stifle your life? Are you tired of doing nothing? Find something God is doing and set to work. He will show you the meaning and purpose in His time.

You are always at work creating Your kingdom
while I have spent too much time idled by fear.
Forgive me for doing nothing. Today I will start
to work in the small tasks where I know You are at
work – among the poor, the needy, the lost. As I work,
affirm in my heart that this is Your work. Amen.

Be Ready for Judgment

God will bring every work into judgment,
including every secret thing, whether good or evil.

~ Ecclesiastes 12:14

Ecclesiastes shows there is much that we will never know about God and His ways. But the book ends by affirming what we can easily know: God's commandments.

Obeying the commandments written in the Word is the first step of obedience. If you do not take the first step, you will face His judgment. What commandment are you not obeying?

You are a God of morality. You make it clear that some things are right and other things are wrong. I know You are right. Still, sometimes I keep wanting to do what I know is wrong. Today I forsake this path of wrong decisions. I choose to obey and experience You. Amen.

Preparing for the Messiah

Therefore the LORD *Himself will give you a sign:*
Behold, the virgin shall conceive and bear a Son,
and shall call His name Immanuel.

~ Isaiah 7:14

Seven hundred years before Jesus was born, God prepared Israel to receive Him, recognize Him, and obey Him. Now almost 2,100 years after Jesus, God still works to help us receive, recognize, and obey Jesus. What excuse are you giving God for not responding to His centuries of work?

Savior, You have worked all the necessary work for my salvation. You have given me all the evidence I need to see You at work in Jesus. I forsake my excuses. I give my life to Jesus. Work Your works through Him in me. Amen.

God Supplies Your Needs

My Well-beloved has a vineyard on a very fruitful hill.

~ Isaiah 5:1

Isaiah told Israel, "You are God's vineyard. He has showered all His love on you to make you productive in His kingdom." But angrily, God listed the faults of the beloved vineyard. Would He react the same way toward you? What fruit are you producing from the love He has showered on you?

Well-beloved, You have worked hard to prepare everything just right for my life. Forgive me that I am not producing what You expect. I turn my life anew and afresh to You. Make me fruitful, Lord. Amen.

God Invites You
to Go Where He Calls

I heard the voice of the Lord, saying: "Whom shall I send, and who will go for Us?" Then I said, "Here am I! Send me."

~ Isaiah 6:8

When God speaks, He never issues an invitation that will not lead to an intimate love relationship with Him if you answer it as Isaiah did. Do you want an intimate walk with God? Listen for His invitation. Be ready to go where He calls.

Master, I stand at Your call. I will go where You say. Any mission I would choose for myself would lead nowhere. Your mission leads me into Your arms of love. Here I am, Lord. Send me! Amen.

June 26

God Speaks Through Your Family

Here am I and the children whom the LORD has given me! We are for signs and wonders in Israel from the LORD of hosts, who dwells on Mount Zion.

~ Isaiah 8:18

Isaiah found that God was revealing Himself through the life of his family. The symbolic names of his children and the example of his family compared to the rest of the community, proclaimed God's glory everywhere Isaiah and his family went. What does your family say about the nature of God just by being present with other people?

Father, You have given me a family. This is part of the way You let me join in Your work. Father, work through my family that we may be signs of who You are and what You are doing in this world. I give my family to be part of Your work. Amen.

June 27

Your Ways or God's Ways?

Let the wicked forsake his way, and the unrighteous man his thoughts; let him return to the LORD, and He will have mercy on him; and to our God, for He will abundantly pardon.

~ Isaiah 55:7

You face a crisis of belief when you know what God wants you to do but you don't do it. One thing God wants you to do is to turn away from any wrong: any bad habit, any fear not surrendered, any ambition that prevents you from making Him Master. Will you stop and tell God what you are going to forsake?

Righteous One, Your pure ways shame me, for my ways are sinful. Somehow I lose the compulsion to please only You. Forgive me, God. Right now I give to You the desires that lead me to sin against You. Amen.

Forsake Wickedness

Is this not the fast that I have chosen: To loose the
bonds of wickedness, to undo the heavy burdens, to let
the oppressed go free, and that you break every yoke?

~ *Isaiah 58:6*

Life adjustments are costly and will be noticed. Your family may notice first. You may act in ways they do not understand: you go out of your way to help people from the wrong social class or you spend money to help others rather than on yourself. What cost are you willing to bear to adjust your life to God's ways?

Friend of the friendless, today I want to become the
person You work through. I will be a friend to the
homeless, share my home with the poor, clothe those who
cannot buy their own clothes. I am Yours. Amen.

Live in God's Light

The sun shall no longer be your light by day, nor for brightness shall the moon give light to you; but the LORD will be to you an everlasting light, and your God your glory.

~ Isaiah 60:19

Allow God to take all the time He needs to shape you for His purposes. He promises that a new day is coming when we shall live forever in the light of His loving presence.

Look forward to that glorious day, but until it comes take the experiences of each day and let God use them to shape your character. Join in this confession of faith and dedication.

Eternal God, mold me into Your image. Help me find in the experiences of today, the things that will make me useable for You. Amen.

July

In Him we have redemption through His blood, the forgiveness of sins, according to the riches of His grace. ~ Ephesians 1:7

God Equips You for Service

The LORD said to me: "Behold, I have put My words in your mouth. See, I have this day set you over the nations and over the kingdoms, to root out and to pull down, to destroy and to throw down, to build and to plant."

~ Jeremiah 1:9-10

When you accepted Him as Lord, you gave Him the right to use your life anytime He wants. Often, He helps Himself by inviting you to a special work for Him and then equipping You to do it. God put His words in Jeremiah's mouth. How has He equipped you to fulfill His mission?

Lord and Master, I am Yours to do with as You please. Equip me to do Your work. I am Your servant, ready to do whatever You demand. Amen.

God Remembers
Your History with Him

*"Go and cry in the hearing of Jerusalem, saying, 'Thus
says the LORD: "I remember you, the kindness of your
youth, the love of your betrothal, when you went after
Me in the wilderness, in a land not sown."'"*

~ Jeremiah 2:2

God has always desired a love relationship with you.
He uses all His efforts to bring this to reality. God
does not desire a casual fling. He has done much
in His courtship of you. He remembers the entire
history of your relationship with Him. He wants to
renew the warmth of those first days together. Do
you?

*Lover, I come back to You. Why did I ever wander away?
Why did I ever think other people and other things could
fill Your place in my life? I am sorry. Let's get back
together in our wonderful love relationship. Amen.*

July 2

God Invites You to Test His People

*"I have set you as an assayer and a fortress among
My people, that you may know and test their way."*

~ Jeremiah 6:27

God had to prove that His people deserved the punishment He was announcing through Jeremiah. Before He acted, God invited Jeremiah to be a testing agent to prove the stubborn ways of the people. Is God inviting you to join Him in a new work? Are you willing – even if the work is one of judgment?

Judge of the universe, I want to be an agent of redemption. Even if You invite me to work as You judge Your people, I will with a sad heart answer the invitation. I want to do whatever You call me to do. Amen.

Obey God's Ways

"This is what I commanded them, saying, 'Obey
My voice, and I will be your God, and you shall be
My people. And walk in all the ways that I have
commanded you, that it may be well with you.'"

~ *Jeremiah 7:23*

From the Exodus on, God had one message for His
people: be My covenant people by walking in My
ways.

Israel failed to obey. Through Jeremiah, God had
to announce the coming of wrath. Do you believe
He will bring wrath if you do not obey His ways?

God of the eternal ways, You have always
called Your people to obey. We have repeatedly
been stubborn, clinging to our own human ways.
I will dare to be different. I pledge my life to an
obedient, love relationship with You. Amen.

July 4

Purchase the Worthless

Then Hanamel my uncle's son came ... and said to me,
"Please buy my field that is in Anathoth, which is in the
country of Benjamin; for the right of inheritance is yours,
and the redemption yours; buy it for yourself." Then I
knew that this was the word of the LORD.

~ Jeremiah 32:8

Jeremiah struggled with the assignment he had been given. He had announced the destruction and capture of the land, which meant all property was worthless. God told him to follow His law and buy property to keep it in his family. Financial advisors would call him foolish. God called him faithful. What does God call you?

Master, human reason advises against joining
in Your work. Faith says, "Plunge ahead."
I will do it Your way. Amen.

Flee From Safety

Move from the midst of Babylon, go out of the land of the Chaldeans; and be like the rams before the flocks.

~ *Jeremiah 50:8*

To Jeremiah's audience God's work seemed to be constantly changing. First, they were told to surrender to Babylon. Then Jeremiah told them God wanted them to leave Babylon.

God's ways are constant, but how He achieves His purposes may vary from situation to situation. Are you ready to adapt to what God is doing today rather than depending on what you heard in the past?

Shepherd of my life, You have blessed me with this wonderful situation. What are You saying? Do You want me to go somewhere else, somewhere not so safe, somewhere that requires risk? I know the only way to work with You is to go where You are working. Let's go. Amen.

July 6

Achieve Your Objective

They said, "We will drink no wine, for Jonadab the son
of Rechab, our father, commanded us, saying, 'You shall
drink no wine, you nor your sons, forever.'"

~ Jeremiah 35:6

The clan of Rechabites found the assignment God had for them. They were to be an example of stubborn faith, clinging to practices of life God showed them to be right.

God honored their faithfulness. Has your family taught you ways to obey God that you know are right? Are you maintaining this faithfulness?

Father, You blessed me with a family that taught
me how to be faithful to You. I will live by Your
rules of life, for only they lead to true life. I will
teach these to my children because I love them and
want them to obey and experience You. Amen.

July 7

God Works in Affliction

*Her adversaries have become the master, her
enemies prosper; for the LORD has afflicted her because
of the multitude of her transgressions. Her children
have gone into captivity before the enemy.*

~ Lamentations 1:5

Israel learned an important lesson rather abruptly when God let Babylon destroy Jerusalem. Israel listened to the prophets and understood that they must adjust to God.

God's work with sinners is to discipline and judge them until they learn that God demands life adjustments. Have you learned this basic lesson?

*God, a love relationship with You is not an on again,
off again affair. I have finally learned the lesson.
Forgive me. Restore me. Amen.*

July 8

God's Faithfulness Renews Hope

*Through the L*ORD*'s mercies we are not consumed, because His*
compassions fail not. They are new every morning;
*great is Your faithfulness. "The L*ORD *is my portion," says*
*my soul, "therefore I hope in Him!" The L*ORD *is good to*
those who wait for Him, to the soul who seeks Him.
~ Lamentations 3:22-25

Israel finally got the message of God's love in their
worst moment. Amid Jerusalem's ashes they saw
that survival remained only because God loved
them. God's faithfulness led to renewed hope for
Israel. What must God do to renew hope in your
life?

Faithful One, how much must You do before
I get the picture? You loved me, died for me,
called me to Yourself, blessed me, and now You
are disciplining me. Thank You, Father. I will
obey You. You are my only hope. Amen.

July 9

Be On Guard for God

"So you, son of man; I have made you a watchman
for the house of Israel; therefore you shall hear a word
from My mouth and warn them for Me."

~ *Ezekiel 33:7*

When we accept God's invitation to join in His work, we also accept responsibility for staying with it until the assignment is fulfilled. God's invitation to Ezekiel put great stress on him. He had to warn the wicked of approaching death or take responsibility for their death.

Ezekiel stuck to the invitation and carried it out. Are you willing to stay with God to the end, or do you only accept invitations for short term assignments?

God, show me how to stay on the course until You
have finished what You started in me. Amen.

God Speaks the Promise of Life

*"Then you shall know that I am the L*ORD*, when
I have opened your graves, O My people, and
brought you up from your graves."*

~ *Ezekiel 37:13*

A spiritual marker identifies a time of transition, decision, or direction when you clearly know that God has guided you. Ezekiel provides a spiritual marker in Scripture, marking Israel's transition from hopeless people in exile to renewed people starting over in the restored Promised Land. How has God revealed to you that He is the Resurrection and the Life?

*Life itself, when I do not obey and experience You,
I walk in the valley of death and miss the excitement
of life. Draw me back to You in obedience so that I may
know life and know it more abundantly. Thank You for
the assurance of resurrection. Amen.*

July 11

Walk in the Spirit

"I will put My Spirit within you and cause you to walk in My statutes, and you will keep My judgments and do them."

~ *Ezekiel 36:27*

The Spirit makes obedience possible. Living in you, the Spirit prompts you to answer God's invitation. Listening to the Spirit always leads to the right decision when you face a crisis of belief.

Spirit of God, live in me. Take away the self-centeredness that makes me ignore You, O Holy Spirit. Bring to pass what You have purposed for me. I love You. Amen.

From Self-Control
to Spirit Control

*"Then you will remember your evil ways and your deeds that
were not good; and you will loathe yourselves in your own
sight, for your iniquities and your abominations."*

~ *Ezekiel 36:31*

God reveals to you where you have disobeyed Him.
He brings a sense of self-loathing; a sense of total
failure. This is only one temporary step. God does
not want you to keep on hating yourself. He wants
you to let His Spirit control your life. This is the
basic adjustment you have to make: from self-control to Spirit control.

*Holy One, You alone can reveal my sin to me. Open my
heart. Bring that godly self-hatred that leads to repentance
and renewal. Send Your Spirit into my life that I can make
the life adjustments You lead me to make. Amen.*

July 13

God Gives Second Chances

"I will make a covenant of peace with them,
and it shall be an everlasting covenant with them;
I will establish them and multiply them and I will
set My sanctuary in their midst forevermore."

~ Ezekiel 37:26

God often gives a second chance. Tracing the history of covenant through Scripture shows how Israel repeatedly got a new chance to experience a new covenant with God, a covenant bringing peace and based on God's work in the hearts of His people. Do you stand in the new covenant? Is He your God?

My Lord, thank You for the second chances You have given me. Again I come to You asking for Your grace to forgive my sin. I feel Your presence and find new assurance that I am part of Your covenant people. Hallelujah. Amen.

July 14

God Answers Prayer

I thank You and praise You, O God of my fathers;
You have given me wisdom and might, and have
now made known to me what we asked of You,
for You have made known to us the king's demand.

~ Daniel 2:23

Daniel and his friends asked for a specific answer to a specific situation of crisis and God answered. They had no idea how He was preparing to speak to them and use them in the months ahead.

Do you see God using an answered prayer to point you towards the God-sized purpose He has for you?

Answerer of prayer, use the Bible, prayer, circumstances, the church, any way You choose to speak to me. Give me the heart of faith to hear and obey. I love You. Amen.

July 15

Mercy for the Obedient

*I prayed to the LORD my God, and made confession,
and said, "O Lord, great and awesome God, who keeps
His covenant and mercy with those who love Him,
and with those who keep His commandments."*

~ *Daniel 9:4*

Daniel repeatedly had encounters with God in obedient prayer. He confessed his sins and the sins of the people. He asked God to renew the relationship.

He admitted that he did not deserve what he asked God, but depended wholly on God's love relationship. What are you asking God for?

*Merciful One, only Your mercy gives us hope. I come to
You to renew my life and bring spiritual awakening to
my community. Begin this work as I repent of my sin
and trust totally in Your mercy. Amen.*

Do You Know God's Vision?

He said, "Look, I am making known to you what
shall happen in the latter time of the indignation;
for at the appointed time the end shall be."

~ Daniel 8:19

God says that if He ever lets His people know what He is about to do, it is as good as done – He Himself will bring it to pass. Daniel saw God's vision for earth's entire life span, from eternity to eternity.

How much of His vision for our world and for your life has God revealed to you? Is God's vision becoming your vision?

Visionary One who controls the destiny of each
individual and holds the entire universe in Your hand,
share Your vision with me. Let me catch a glimpse
of what You are about to do. Show me the part I can
play in bringing that vision to reality. Give me the
excitement to share Your vision with others. Amen.

July 17

Interpret God's Word

In the first year of his reign I, Daniel, understood by the books
the number of the years specified by the word of the LORD
through Jeremiah the prophet, that He would accomplish
seventy years in the desolation of Jerusalem.

~ Daniel 9:2

Watch to see how God may use truth about Himself
from a Bible verse you read today. See if He uses it
in your life today. Daniel found new understanding
about God's purposes in the words of Jeremiah. Are
you reading God's Word daily, seeking truth about
Him and His purposes?

Author of the eternal Word, speak to me. Use the book
of Daniel to teach me Your eternal truth. Amen.

God or Government?

If you do not worship, you shall be cast immediately into the midst of a burning fiery furnace. And who is the god who will deliver you from my hands?

~ Daniel 3:15

Daniel's friends faced a God-sized choice: believe the government or believe God. Government offered food, shelter, and rescue from death. God offered an invisible protection from life's problems and hope for life beyond.

Human wisdom had no problem making the choice. Faith faced a crisis. How do you respond today when God's ways contradict sound economic advice?

Giver of all I have, You know my present economic situation. The world has a way for me to get out but I want Your way. Show it to me today. Amen.

July 19

God's Lifestyle

Daniel purposed in his heart that he would not defile himself with the portion of the king's delicacies, nor with the wine which he drank; therefore he requested of the chief of the eunuchs that he might not defile himself.

~ Daniel 1:8

Daniel found that one small life adjustment was only the beginning of an adventure with God. Daniel's first adjustment really involved no changes. It simply reconfirmed his commitment to the ways of God he had always followed. New circumstances required this new commitment. Will you commit yourself anew to God's way?

Help me, God. I face new challenges. People want to convince me that a new way of life is necessary in today's world. God, I refuse to do it their way. I want to do it Your way. Amen.

July 20

God Delivers

If that is the case, our God whom we serve is able to deliver us from the burning fiery furnace, and He will deliver us from your hand, O king.

~ Daniel 3:17

Daniel's friends had done everything they thought possible to be faithful to God. Suddenly, the king said, "Sin or die." The young men said, "If that is the way it must be, so be it. Death is a better option than sin."

Have you been disappointed in the way things have worked out for you and decided that God's will is leading nowhere? Think again. God is in the business of delivering from dead-end streets.

Deliverer, I am at wits' end. Still, I want to be true to You. Show me again the glory of experience with You even when life seems to close all doors. Amen.

July 21

God-Centered Plans

She did not know that I gave her grain, new wine, and oil,
and multiplied her silver and gold – which they prepared for Baal.

~ Hosea 2:8

Israel got so accustomed to doing things their own way that they entirely forgot God's way. God gave the gifts, but Israel gave them to idols. They thought they were being good servants of God.

What resources has God given you that you are using for your own selfish plans – like vacations, football games, shopping sprees? Will you put self-centered plans aside for God-centered plans?

Giver of every good gift, help me make a list of
activities I must eliminate from my self-centered life
so I can concentrate on God-centered work. Amen.

Divine Bridegroom

"I will betroth you to Me in faithfulness,
and you shall know the LORD."

~ Hosea 2:20

If for some reason you cannot think of a time when your relationship with God has been real, personal, and practical, you need to spend some time evaluating your relationship to Him.

Hosea said the love relationship with God is more intimate than that between husband and wife. It is a blend of two persons committed to one another in righteousness, love, mercy, and faithfulness. Is your relationship to God that real?

My Heavenly Mate, we have pledged vows of love to one another. Too often that pledge has been awfully one-sided. Today that changes. I will be faithful to You above all other allegiances. Thank You, Lord, for loving me. Amen.

God Invites You
to Return to Him

*O Israel, return to the L*ORD *your God, for you*
have stumbled because of your iniquity; take
*words with you, and return to the L*ORD.

~ *Hosea 14:1-2*

Spiritual awakening begins only as believers face God's discipline for sin and cry out to God in repentance. Will you join those thousands today who are confessing sins explicitly to God and finding His love anew? Will you return to Him and see your iniquity taken away?

Forgiver of sin, You know my sin, but I need to
confess it to You. Take away my laziness, my lust,
my lack of commitment, my loyalties to things rather
than to You. I return to You and pray for spiritual
awakening in our church and in our city today. Amen.

Love the Unlovely

Then the LORD said to me, "Go again, love a woman who is loved by a lover and is committing adultery, just like the love of the LORD for the children of Israel, who look to other gods and love the raisin cakes of the pagans."

~ Hosea 3:1

God told Hosea, "You must have a forgiving heart with My kind of forgiveness. You must forgive a wife who has betrayed you." That is a God-sized task, but it reveals the God-sized nature of His love. Are you willing to act on faith to accomplish a God-sized task that shows a God-sized love?

Love! That is Your nature. You want me to be like that. I will do it. I will love as You love. Help me begin with one person today. Amen.

In Desperate Days

Consecrate a fast, call a sacred assembly; gather the elders and all the inhabitants of the land into the house of the LORD your God, and cry out to the LORD.

~ Joel 1:14

Israel had reached the end of the rope. They had no resources for victory. God had brought judgment on His people. Joel responded to the crisis by calling the people to public lament in God's house. What response do you make to hopeless situations where God is obviously disciplining you?

Destroyer of all evil, the end has come. I will go to God's people in Your house. Together we will call on Your mercy. We repent and will come out of this crisis with new faith and new obedience. Amen.

July 26

Obey the Spirit

"It shall come to pass afterward that I will pour out My
Spirit on all flesh; your sons and your daughters shall
prophesy, your old men shall dream dreams, your young
men shall see visions. And also on My menservants and on
My maidservants I will pour out My Spirit in those days."

~ Joel 2:28-29

Joel promised a day when all God's people would
have God's Holy Spirit directing their lives. Acts
tells of the Day of Pentecost when the promise came
true. The Spirit brought extraordinary adjustments
to the lives of the early church. How is your life
different because the Spirit lives in You?

Holy Spirit, come dwell in me. Take charge of
my life. Fine-tune me until I am a perfect running
instrument carrying out Your will. Amen.

Experience God's Salvation

It shall come to pass that whoever calls on the name of the LORD shall be saved. For in Mount Zion and in Jerusalem there shall be deliverance, as the LORD has said, among the remnant whom the LORD calls.

~ Joel 2:32

Joel called to Israel in the darkest of days and promised saving light on the other side. He admitted only a remnant would come through, a remnant who called in faith for God's salvation. Will you call on Him for salvation now?

Deliverer, why do I have such a hard time believing Your promise? Give me faith. I will call on You and know You are bringing salvation. O, Lord, in obeying You I experience You. Amen.

God Brings Judgment

"You only have I known of all the families of the earth;
therefore, I will punish you for all your iniquities."

~ *Amos 3:2*

God pursues an intimate relationship, choosing to do His work through certain people He loves. But what happens when those people refuse to return God's love or join in His work, or pile up a storehouse of sins in their lives? God has only one choice left. He comes to punish.

Amos had a hard time convincing Israel of this. Does God have a hard time convincing you that He is coming to judge and punish?

Judge of all the earth, You judge because we refuse to love and obey You. I have chosen self-centered ways and not God-centered ways. Forgive me. I am repenting of my sin. I am listening to Your voice. I am going to obey You and experience You in love, not punishment. Amen.

Mercy Instead of Punishment

"O Lord God, forgive, I pray! Oh, that Jacob may
stand, for he is small!" So the Lord relented
concerning this. "It shall not be," said the Lord.

~ *Amos 7:2-3*

When your relationship is as it ought to be, you will always be in fellowship with the Father. But what happens when that relationship is not what it ought to be? Then you and the church need to pray to God not to bring punishment.

Amos found that God listened to such prayers and withheld His punishment. But such prayers must be accompanied by obedience. Are you willing to obey so God will not renew His judgment?

Merciful One, Your mercy is my only hope.
We have sinned. We deserve Your punishment,
but we pray for Your mercy. Give us another
chance to obey You and experience Your love. Amen.

July 30

Listen to the Shepherd

*Then the LORD took me as I followed the flock, and the
LORD said to me, "Go, prophesy to My people Israel."*

~ Amos 7:15

A tender and sensitive heart will be ready to respond to God at the slightest prompting. Amos led his animals from pasture to pasture, depending on God to show him where to take them. Then God called with a bigger task: shepherd My people to their doom.

Amos had no qualifications for the job but God invited Him. So Amos went to work with God. Are you waiting until you have the credentials to do God's work? Or do you simply listen for God's voice?

*Shepherd of my life, I want to hear and follow
Your voice. Make clear today the work I can do
for You. Be with me and guide me as I do it.
Whatever You say, I will do. Amen.*

July 31

August

The LORD shall preserve you; He shall preserve your soul.
The LORD shall preserve your going out and your coming
in from this time forth, and even forevermore. ~ Psalm 121:7-8

God Does Not Forget

The L{\sc ord} has sworn by the pride of Jacob:
"Surely I will never forget any of their works."

~ Amos 8:7

When God speaks by the Holy Spirit to you, He often reveals something about Himself. God revealed part of His character to Amos: He does not forget unconfessed sins. Are you, like Israel, complacent and confident in your relationship with God because of all the good things you have done in the past? Are you forgetting unconfessed sins that God never forgets?

Pride of Jacob, the only source of pride I could ever have, I come to You in confession. I have become complacent, too self-confident in my relationship with You. Teach me again that I cannot earn my way to heaven. I must rely only on Your grace. I confess my sins and pledge anew to listen and obey You. Amen.

August 1

Service or Ritual?

"Offer a sacrifice of thanksgiving with leaven,
proclaim and announce the freewill offerings;
for this you love, you children of Israel!"

~ Amos 4:5

Israel enjoyed unprecedented success, and their good life brought good income for the priests. Everyone was happy, except God. He hated Israel's offerings and worship rituals, because they were self-centered, not God-centered. Is your worship service to praise God or a ritual to please people?

God who knows me, too easily I worship as
I have always done, seeking to get something out
of it for myself, thinking I can look good before the
people. I know it does not work that way. Accept
my sacrifice of praise and humility. Amen.

Seek God, Not Tradition

"Take away from Me the noise of your songs, for I will not hear the melody of your stringed instruments. But let justice run down like water, and righteousness like a mighty stream."

~ *Amos 5:23-24*

Israel had a problem: they thought they knew what to do without consulting God. They had the right songs to sing, the right actions to take in worship. What they had done for centuries, they kept doing.

God called a halt to worship. He demanded right living before right singing. Has following the way of the church become more important to you than following the ways of God?

God of justice, make me an instrument of Your loving care and justice instead of just an instrument in the choir. Amen.

God's Kingdom

Then saviors shall come to Mount Zion to judge the mountains of Esau, and the kingdom shall be the LORD's.

~ *Obadiah 21*

When you obey Him, you have to allow Him to do what He has said. He is the one who accomplishes the assignment, but He does it through you. Israel wanted to defeat Edom's army and occupy territory. Obadiah promised them Edom would lose out, but the fight would be done God's way. Are you working God's way to establish His kingdom, or your way to establish your kingdom?

King of all the earth and General of all the armies, let Your kingdom come and Your will be done here on earth. I want to be a part of Your strategy. I want to forsake the self-centered strategy I have been following. Command me, Lord. I will follow orders. Amen.

August 4

God Protects His Prophets

*The LORD spoke to the fish,
and it vomited Jonah onto dry land.*

~ *Jonah 2:10*

God always develops character to match his assignments. If God has a great assignment for you, He has to develop a great character before He can give you the assignment.

Jonah had to learn this the hard way, and still did not learn very well. What does it take for God to shape you so you are ready for His assignment?

Master Builder, build me. Repair everything about me until I am fit for the assignments You want to give me. Tear out from me all that would hinder me from doing Your work. Insert into me everything necessary to accomplish Your will. I love You. Amen.

Have Pity for People

Should I not pity Nineveh, that great city,
in which are more than one hundred and twenty
thousand persons who cannot discern between their
right hand and their left – and much livestock?

~ Jonah 4:11

Jonah lived in an atmosphere of hatred for the Assyrians who had power over Israel. God showed Jonah His strategy for Assyria and its capital city of Nineveh.

God chose to reveal His love and call Assyria to repentance. Spiritual awakening in Nineveh fulfilled God's purpose but made Jonah mad. Are there places and people you do not want to know God's love?

Lover of my enemies, teach me to love them. Enhance
my capacity for love. Give me Your perspective on
people and Your care for the lost. Amen.

Witness to the Wicked

"Arise, go to Nineveh, that great city, and cry out against it;
for their wickedness has come up before Me."

~ *Jonah 1:2*

Jonah received God's "mission impossible". Go to
a foreign nation's capital, that controls the political
destiny of your nation, and tell them how wicked
they are. Is that a God-sized task?

Jonah was not ready for it. He had too much hate,
too little love, and too much pride. What prevents
you from accepting God-sized invitations?

Ruler of all the universe, my own nation looks
like Nineveh: immoral, power-hungry, full of
hatred against different groups. God, do I hear
You forming a God-sized invitation to cry out about
the wickedness of this nation? Amen.

August 7

God Gives Direction

They said to one another, "Come, let us cast lots, that we may know for whose cause this trouble has come upon us." So they cast lots, and the lot fell on Jonah.

~ *Jonah 1:7*

Only God can give you specific directions to accomplish His purposes in His ways. God used pagan sailors to deal with disobedient Jonah.

If His ways are available in a specific situation to pagan sailors, do you think He is capable and will give you specific directions for life?

Leader in every situation of life, speak to me today. You know the situation I have gotten myself into. Now I recognize how drastically I need You, not only in this situation, but in every situation of life. I wait for You to speak so I can know how to get out of this mess and obey and experience You. Amen.

August 8

Preach or Perish

*"Arise, go to Nineveh, that great city, and
preach to it the message that I tell you."*

~ *Jonah 3:2*

Jonah carried out God's call to preach with reluctance. He preached five Hebrew words. Then he waited to make sure God destroyed Nineveh as He had promised, fearful God would give the enemy a second chance.

Crisis of belief calls for full commitment to the task, not a commitment based on fear of consequences but on dedication to God and His work.

*Gracious and merciful God, I am tempted to volunteer
for work that reflects my own feelings. Show me
anew Your work, overcoming all pride and prejudice
to help those who need You most. Your love for others,
even for my enemies, is not something I resent. It is
something I want to join You in. Help me. Amen.*

August 9

Care for the Enemy

God said to Jonah, "Is it right for you to
be angry about the plant?" And he said, "It
is right for me to be angry, even to death!"

~ *Jonah 4:9*

Jonah could repeat the creed about God's love, but then he resented that God loved so much. Jonah wanted to depend on one side of God's character, His judgment of sin, and ignore the loving side of God. Do you want to use part of God to do your will rather than let God be free to determine what is best in the situation?

Master, I do not really want to let You be Master.
I have parts of my life I want You to master and
parts I want to keep hold of. Help me to quit
depending on me and my will, and start turning
everything over to You and Your love. Amen.

August 10

Obey and Experience God Through Repentance

The people of Nineveh believed God, proclaimed a fast,
and put on sackcloth, from the greatest to the least of them.

~ Jonah 3:5

Jonah wanted God for himself, not for the Assyrians. But God used even the reluctant Jonah to lead the Assyrians to obey and experience Him through repentance, fasting, and mourning.

Meanwhile, Jonah bawled God out for being so loving. Who are you like: the repentant Assyrians or reluctant, self-centered Jonah? Are you experiencing God?

Universal God, too many times I want to localize You.
But You want to universalize me, send me to the ends
of the earth to share Your love or bring the ends of the
earth to my doorstep so I can share with them here. Be
Thou my vision, so I will love the world as You do and
be glad to do the universal work You are doing. Amen.

August 11

God Is Just

The LORD is righteous in her midst, He will do no unrighteousness. Every morning He brings His justice to light; He never fails, but the unjust know no shame.

~ Zephaniah 3:5

Israel could not learn God's basic principle: imitate God in His justice and righteousness. They let wealth and leisure set standards instead of God. God never changes. He does justice always, every day. Do you work like God or like Israel?

Righteous One, Your consistency amazes me. My actions are not like that. I try to protect myself, make sure I get a fair shake. But no one ever promised me life would be fair. You did promise that from Your eternal perspective I would receive grace. Thank You for Your consistent mercy in spite of my inconsistent commitment. Amen.

August 12

Trust in God

*The L*ORD *is good, a stronghold in the day of trouble;*
and He knows those who trust in Him.

~ Nahum 1:7

In the midst of despair Judah received Nahum's word from God: God is good; you can trust Him; He knows personally those who trust Him; He will protect you in the worst of times; He will defeat your enemies. Do you trust God to do what is good for you?

Good, that is what You are, God. Evil can claim
no part of You. In Your goodness You love me.
You want good for me. That is what a love relationship
is all about, wanting good for one another.
I surrender my despair. I have hope. Amen.

God Invites You to a Life without Fear

"According to the word that I covenanted with you when you came out of Egypt, so My Spirit remains among you; do not fear."

~ Haggai 2:5

Haggai saw a disgruntled people living in fear before conquering enemies. He called Israel to take their eyes off the enemies and put them on God.

Who had the most power? Who would live eternally? Who ultimately controlled the world and all its destinies? What promise had God ever failed to keep? As for you, what are you afraid of? Why?

Fear of Israel, I have no reason to fear. In a love relationship with You, everything will turn out right. Still, I fear my boss, failure, the opinions of other people, the darkness, what tomorrow might bring. Take these fears away. Let me hear Your word of promise. I will fear no evil. You are with me. Amen.

August 14

God Reveals the Spirit's Power

Truly I am full of power by the Spirit of the LORD, and of justice and might, to declare to Jacob his transgression and to Israel his sin.

~ Micah 3:8

Spiritual truths can be revealed only by God, but sin blinds us to God. The Spirit reveals to us our sin so we can adjust our lives to God's work and see His purposes.

To be filled with the Spirit means to be filled with justice and power. How has the Spirit revealed your sin? Are you experiencing God's power in what you do?

Spirit of the holy God, guide me into God's work and let me do it with power and justice. Spirit, only as I hear Your voice can I experience God in obedience, doing His work. Come, Holy Spirit, come to me today. Amen.

August 15

Faith or Pride?

Behold the proud, his soul is not upright in him;
but the just shall live by his faith.

~ *Habakkuk 2:4*

Habakkuk was full of questions for God. How could God possibly use a wicked nation like Babylon to punish Israel? God said, "Do not let pride prevent you from seeing what I am doing. You must live faithfully each day, trusting that I know what I am doing."

Do you have a lot of questions for God? Are you willing to trust Him and wait until He is ready to answer your questions?

Upright One, I trust You. But sometimes it is
awfully hard with so many questions dancing in
my head. Give me patience to live each day obediently
experiencing Your love. Teach me to trust You
with questions I cannot answer. Amen.

August 16

Complete the Task

*Thus says the L*ORD *of hosts: "Let your hands be strong, you who have been hearing in these days these words by the mouth of the prophets, who spoke in the day the foundation was laid for the house of the L*ORD *of hosts, that the temple might be built."*

~ Zechariah 8:9

Zechariah faced an unbelieving audience. He really expected this poor bunch without hope to start building God's temple one more time. Why try again? Because God said so. Will you change your attitude and your ways simply because God says to?

Lord of Hosts, help me take You at Your word. Help me simply accept, "Because I said so," as reason enough to trust You. Lord, You know that is hard for me. But I will do it Your way. Amen.

August 17

Turning People from Sin

*"The law of truth was in his mouth, and injustice was not
found on his lips. He walked with Me in peace and equity,
and turned many away from iniquity."*

~ *Malachi 2:6*

God had trouble bringing His priests to the next
steps of maturity. So God promised a new day with
new priests and new obedience.

Turned away from sin, the people could then
turn others away from it. Is your life turning people
to or away from sin?

*Pure and perfect One, You want a pure witness to other
people so that You can work through me to turn them
away from sin and to You. I want to be that kind of
person so I can obey and experience You. Amen.*

August 18

God Fulfills the Scriptures

All this was done that it might be fulfilled which
was spoken by the Lord through the prophet.

~ Matthew 1:22

How do you let the Word of God become your guide? The New Testament church found this to be the burning question for them. They had the Old Testament, proven true over the years, as the perfect Word of God. Now they had Jesus.

How did they put Scripture and Jesus together? They found that the work God did in Jesus was the very work He promised to do in the Old Testament. Does God continue to do what He promised to do in the Bible?

Fulfiller of all Scripture You inspired, use Your Word to work in my life today. Thank You that You used Scripture to prepare us for Jesus. Now use Scripture to prepare me to do Your work. Amen.

August 19

God Loves My Enemies

"I say to you, love your enemies, bless those who curse you, do good to those who hate you, and pray for those who spitefully use you and persecute you, that you may be sons of your Father in heaven."

~ Matthew 5:44-45

God does not determine whether you deserve His love before He loves you. Likewise, He does not want you to set up a test others must pass before you can love them. He wants you to love them and pray for them no matter how they treat you. How many people do you need to add to your love list and your prayer list today?

God, teach me to love as You love. I will begin praying for those I do not like right now. My first prayer is to love them. Amen.

August 20

Follow God

As Jesus passed on from there, He saw a man named
Matthew sitting at the tax office. And He said to him,
"Follow Me." So he arose and followed Him.

~ *Matthew 9:9*

The moment God speaks to you is the very moment
He wants you to respond to Him. Jesus did not give
the disciples thirty days' notice to get their house in
order, consider all consequences, and then decide
to follow Him. He said, "Follow." They left all and
followed. How long do you think you have to wait
before answering His invitation?

Lord Jesus, I will follow You. No more waiting
for the right moment. No more trying to get all
circumstances lined up right. You love me. I love You.
I want to follow wherever You are. Amen.

God Speaks in Your Persecution

"When they deliver you up, do not worry about how or what you should speak. For it will be given to you in that hour what you should speak; for it is not you who speak, but the Spirit of your Father who speaks in you."

~ Matthew 10:19-20

Planning is not all wrong. Just be careful not to plan more than God intends for you to plan. Let God interrupt or redirect your plans any time He wants.

When you are in a close, intimate love relationship with God, His Spirit speaks through you. Do you believe this? Are you willing to test it in real-life situations?

Protecting Spirit, give me faith to live as You direct each day so the world will oppose me. Give me words to speak when the world opposes me. Give me testimony to You after the world opposes me. I am Yours and Yours alone. Amen.

August 22

Accept Condemnation

*"Behold, I send you out as sheep in the midst of wolves.
Therefore be as wise as serpents and harmless as doves."*

~ Matthew 10:16

Describe a time in your life that required faith in God and you responded in faith. This would be a time when you could see no way to accomplish the task unless God did it through you.

What required more faith: facing those who said you could not succeed in the work God gave or believing God could accomplish it through you? How did God equip you to face opposition? Did you find God's wisdom when you needed it?

*Strongest of the strong, help me face opposition
with Your strength. Thank You for working in
spite of my weakness. I will do the God-sized
work You call me to. Amen.*

God Before Family

"He who loves father or mother more than Me is not worthy of Me. And he who loves son or daughter more than Me is not worthy of Me. And he who does not take his cross and follow after Me is not worthy of Me."

~ Matthew 10:37-38

List four areas in which God has asked you to make an adjustment of your life to Him. Which one is most difficult for you? Is it setting priorities your family does not like? Is it letting a child do God's will rather than yours? Is it giving up a lifestyle you think you earned so that you can do what God invites you to do?

Adjuster of my life, Your adjustments make my life different from what I dreamed it would be. But You adjusted Your life to die on a cross. I love You enough to make the adjustments You are asking for. Amen.

August 24

Faith and Worship

Then she came and worshiped Him, saying, "Lord, help me!"
~ Matthew 15:25

Jesus tried His best to discourage the Gentile woman. But she refused to be discouraged. Jesus exclaimed amazement at her faith. You too, can have such faith. Faith that leads you to worship Jesus, brings you into the Kingdom. Do you have that faith? Then you will experience God.

Lord, I have faith in You. I trust You with my life.
I will let nothing and no one come between us. I am
not worthy of Your love, but I accept Your love and
return Your love. Save me, loving Lord. Amen.

God Defeats the Demonic

Jesus rebuked the demon, and it came out of him;
and the child was cured from that very hour.

~ Matthew 17:18

Jesus ministered on earth for three short years, yet He changed the course of history and began the kingdom of God on earth. He showed that demonic powers did not control the world. God is sovereign over all countries and all situations. He can work His purposes over all opposition. Do you believe this? How do you let Him defeat the demonic and evil in your life?

Sovereign God, I simply want to praise You today.
You are all-powerful, all-knowing, ever-present,
and all-caring. In gratitude and love I praise You
for the great work You do in establishing Your
kingdom on earth as it is in heaven. Amen.

August 26

Love in Action

They said to Him, "Lord, that our eyes may be opened."
So Jesus had compassion and touched their eyes. And
immediately their eyes received sight, and they followed Him.

~ Matthew 20:33-34

A love relationship with God takes place between two real beings. Jesus constantly found someone to love, usually someone the rest of the world ignored.

Blind people, thought to only be able to sit and beg, Jesus loved with all His compassion. Have you experienced that love? Are you following Him?

Healer of blind eyes, open my blind heart. Too
long I have followed self-centered worldly ways.
You have revealed a God-centered way of love for
all people. I will quit assessing the qualifications of
people before I decide to love them. I will let Your
love flow through me to them. Amen.

God Invites You to
Do the Impossible

Jesus answered and said to them, "Assuredly, I say to you, if you have faith and do not doubt, you will not only do what was done to the fig tree, but also if you say to this mountain, 'Be removed and be cast into the sea,' it will be done. And whatever things you ask in prayer, believing, you will receive."

~ Matthew 21:21-22

We have never experienced all the power of prayer because we place so many limits on prayer. When you take the limits off, God will overwhelm you with the power He lets flow through you to accomplish His work. Dare you ask the impossible?

Miracle-worker, take away the limits I have placed on You with my unbelief. I want You to move mountains in my world today. I believe You are doing it now. Amen.

August 28

God Speaks for Eternity

"Heaven and earth will pass away, but My
words will by no means pass away."

~ *Matthew 24:35*

Every word God speaks prepares for His future, for eternity. You live in the world of the temporary. You expect to have things for a little while and then replace them with something new and better.

God's Word was perfect when first spoken and remains perfect. It never needs replacing. It continues to reveal God, His ways, and His purposes. Are you listening and learning?

Eternal Word, speak to me. I want to know You.
My life is too centered on the temporary and
passing. Show me the eternal that I may build my
life on things everlasting. Amen.

To Betray or to Trust

When evening had come, He sat down with the twelve.
Now, as they were eating, He said, "Assuredly,
I say to you, one of you will betray Me."

~ Matthew 26:20-21

The disciples kept looking for Jesus to establish a kingdom on earth in which they had positions of authority. Finally, Judas saw this was not going to happen and betrayed Jesus. In the end, following his own belief rather than God's ways led to suicide.

Are you slow to believe Jesus and obey Him because you have already decided how things should work out in the world?

Savior, You surprised the world by being
a suffering servant Messiah and not a military
monarch Messiah. Forgive me when I try to decide
how You should work and then am disappointed
that You do not work that way. I am willing to
forsake my way and follow Yours. Amen.

August 30

Being a Servant

*"Yet it shall not be so among you; but whoever desires
to become great among you, let him be your servant. And
whoever desires to be first among you, let him be your slave."*

~ Matthew 20:26-27

Matthew had to forsake security and money to follow Jesus. He must have thought twice when Jesus defined the roles of His followers. Did Matthew want to be a slave forever? That was God's way in God's Kingdom.

Every Kingdom citizen had to serve every other one. Are you being a slave for Jesus? Are you expecting the slave status to be temporary?

*Boss of all the world, I am Your slave. I have
no ambitions to be anything else. You give orders,
and I will obey. Thank You for the privilege of
being a slave in Your Kingdom. That is better
than ruling any other kingdom. Amen.*

August 31

September

*"For God so loved the world that He gave His
only begotten Son, that whoever believes in Him should
not perish but have everlasting life." ~ John 3:16*

Obeying God's Instructions

*As they went to tell His disciples, behold, Jesus
met them, saying, "Rejoice!" So they came and held
Him by the feet and worshiped Him. Then Jesus said to
them, "Do not be afraid. Go and tell My brethren to
go to Galilee, and there they will see Me."*

~ Matthew 28:9-10

One of the disciples' great blessings was participating in the Resurrection experience. But the resurrected Christ sent them on a mission and tested
their faith to see if they would follow instructions.
Are you following Christ's instructions, or are you
doing things your way?

*Resurrected Lord, Your death and resurrection
have given me salvation. Now You want to speak
to me with instructions on how to obey and
experience You. I will listen. Amen.*

September 1

God Baptizes with the Spirit

*I indeed baptized you with water, but He will
baptize you with the Holy Spirit.*

~ *Mark 1:8*

The key to knowing God's voice is not a formula or a method you can follow. You are going to have to watch to see how God uniquely communicates with you. John the Baptist let God speak through him to communicate the mission of the One whose way he prepared.

Jesus' mission was to give you the Holy Spirit so God could speak to you. Are you listening to that Spirit to discover where God is at work?

*Holy Spirit of God, You are always at work in the
heart of Your people to guide us to the work the
Father is doing. Help me to be attentive to Your
voice. In Your own unique way make me aware of
Your mission for me. Amen.*

September 2

Loving God and Your Neighbor

"You shall love the Lord *your God with all your heart,*
with all your soul, with all your mind, and with all your
strength. This is the first commandment. And the second,
like it, is this: 'You shall love your neighbor as yourself.'
There is no other commandment greater than these."

~ Mark 12:30-31

Everything in your Christian life depends on the
quality of your love relationship with God. If that
is not right, nothing in your life will be right. On
a scale of 1 to 10, 1 as unloving and 10 as absolute
love for God, where do you rank?

I have seen Your love in the life and especially
in the death of Your Son, Jesus Christ. Come
again to me today, Lord. Revive and revitalize
our love relationship. Amen.

September 3

Pray Away From Temptation

*"Watch and pray, lest you enter into temptation.
The spirit indeed is willing, but the flesh is weak."*

~ Mark 14:38

Obedience is the outward expression of your love of God. If you have an obedience problem, you have a love problem. Mark's Gospel gives us a picture of the love problems of the disciples. They kept arguing over who was to be first in the Kingdom.

They slept while Jesus prayed in Gethsemane, even after He invited them to pray with Him. How are you answering Christ's invitation to pray to the Father so you can deepen your love relationship with Him?

*Lord Jesus, temptation is so real. My only
hope is to have a strong love relationship with You
that leads me not into temptation and delivers
me from evil. God, as You led Jesus to deal
with Satan's temptations, so help me. Amen.*

September 4

God Speaks Through the Empty Tomb

*Entering the tomb, they saw a young man clothed in
a long white robe sitting on the right side; and they
were alarmed. But he said to them, "Do not be alarmed.
You seek Jesus of Nazareth, who was crucified. He is risen!
He is not here. See the place where they laid Him."*

~ Mark 16:5-6

Perplexed women went to the tomb to do their best in a horrible circumstance. Suddenly, a young messenger showed them the light of new meaning in those desperate circumstances. Are you looking at your circumstances through the light of the resurrection?

*Resurrected One, You give hope to every situation
and circumstance. Teach me to see that hope. Amen.*

September 5

Cross or Crown?

*He said to them, "Whoever desires to come after Me, let
him deny himself, and take up his cross, and follow Me.
For whoever desires to save his life will lose it, but whoever
loses his life for My sake and the gospel's will save it."*

~ Mark 8:34-35

What the world often sees in our day is a devoted
Christian serving God. But they are not seeing God.
Why? Because we are not attempting anything only
God can do. Only God takes up the cross and dies
for others. What are you doing for the world to see
God at work?

*Suffering Servant, You died for my sins and call me
to live for You. Help me understand what that means.
Do a work through me that only You can do. Amen.*

September 6

Become Christ's Servant

"Yet it shall not be so among you; but whoever desires to become great among you shall be your servant. And whoever of you desires to be first shall be slave of all."

~ Mark 10:43-44

A servant is a person who has to do two things: be moldable and remain in the Master's (Potter's) hands. Then the Master alone can use that instrument as He chooses. Are you moldable and staying in the Potter's hands? How is God using You? What is He accomplishing through you?

Master Potter, when I am master, the plan is too small and the result has too little meaning. When You are Master, the plan is universal and the result beyond belief. Mold me in Your eternal plan. Amen.

September 7

Give All You Have

*He called His disciples to Himself and said to them,
"Assuredly, I say to you that this poor widow has put in
more than all those who have given to the treasury; for they
all put in out of their abundance, but she out of her
poverty put in all that she had, her whole livelihood."*

~ Mark 12:43-44

Obedience means joy and uninterrupted fellowship
with God. Our world limits joy to those who have
worldly means to live the good life. Christ limits joy
to those who have the obedience to give away all
they have to enjoy Him. Which kind of joy do you
seek?

*Giver of every good and perfect gift, I know money
cannot buy joy. Yet I cling to what I have. Teach me to
give so that I may obey and experience You. Amen.*

September 8

God Heals and Forgives

"That you may know that the Son of Man has power on earth to forgive sins" – He said to the man who was paralyzed, *"I say to you, arise, take up your bed, and go to your house."*

~ Luke 5:24

God is at work healing helpless people and forgiving sinners. If you, your church, or the activities you participate in do not include helping the helpless and forgiving the sinful, then you may not be where God is working. What do you think?

Forgiver of my sins, all around I see people who need forgiveness, acceptance, and a second chance. Place me beside them, offering the kind of help You alone offer. Make me like You so that I can do the loving work You do. Amen.

God Shows Mercy

"Love your enemies, do good, and lend, hoping for nothing in return; and your reward will be great, and you will be sons of the Most High. For He is kind to the unthankful and evil. Therefore be merciful, just as your Father also is merciful."

~ Luke 6:35-36

Make sure you are investing in things that are lasting. You need to store up treasures in heaven. Heaven's bank accepts only deposits of mercy, not deposits of gold. What does your account balance look like?

Eternal Love, I keep trying to keep up with the competition here and hold on to a little bit of heaven too. Show me I cannot do both. Eternal things will be my only priority. Amen.

Tell What God Has Done for You

"Return to your own house, and tell what great things God has done for you."

~ *Luke 8:39*

When we read the Bible, we are reading the redemptive activity of God in our world. We see that He chooses to invite His people to work with Him.

He begins by sending a person home to share good news with people you know best. Does every person in your family know the good news of God's work?

Father, I too, am a parent. I keep looking for ways to do Your work in my town, on mission trips, or perhaps to hear a call to faraway places. Use me first to tell my children, my spouse, my parents, all my home people about You and Your redemptive work. Amen.

September 11

God Speaks About His Son

A voice came out of the cloud, saying,
"This is My beloved Son. Hear Him!"

~ Luke 9:35

In the Gospel accounts, God was in Christ Jesus. He spoke through Jesus. When the disciples heard Jesus, they heard God. When Jesus spoke, that was an encounter with God. God wants you to recognize Jesus as His Son, the Savior of the world. Are you listening to Jesus? What kind of relationship do you have with Him?

Jesus, You are the Savior of the world. You died that I might have eternal life, now and in the world to come. Jesus, eternal life means listening to Your word and obeying You. Teach me that obedience today. Amen.

September 12

Facing Failure in God's Work

I implored Your disciples to cast it out, but they could not.
~ Luke 9:40

On their own, the disciples could not feed the multitudes, heal the sick, still a storm, or raise the dead. But God called servants to let Him do these things through them. The disciples often failed to do what Jesus wanted them to because they lacked faith to let God work through them. Pentecost finally brought the Spirit and the faith. Are you waiting for God to give you the Spirit and faith you need to do His work?

Lord, I have failed. I have tried to do Your work
in my power. I finally see that without Your Spirit
working through me, I can accomplish nothing.
Increase my faith. Fill me with Your Spirit. I want
to do Your work for Your glory. Amen.

September 13

Lambs Among Wolves

"Go your way; behold, I send you
out as lambs among wolves."

~ Luke 10:3

Obedience requires total dependence on God to work through you. Jesus described you as a totally dependent, helpless, straying lamb. He described your environment as full of ravenous wolves, waiting to catch you. The world has taught you to become independent, ready to manipulate others for your advantage. Are you willing to let God mold your life so that you become a helpless lamb?

Shepherd of the flock, You have called me to
be Your lamb, totally dependent on You and a
prey for all the world to feed on. This is not what
I have been trained to be. It is not the self image
I have of myself. Adjust my life. Make me a lamb
following You, the Good Shepherd. Amen.

September 14

Experience God in Prayer

Now it came to pass, as He was praying in a certain place,
when He ceased, that one of His disciples said to Him,
"Lord, teach us to pray, as John also taught his disciples."

~ Luke 11:1

After you pray, the greatest single thing you need to do is turn on your spiritual concentration. When you pray in a direction, immediately anticipate the activity of God in answer to your prayer. How do you experience God's answer to prayer? Do you see Him at work answering prayer? Is that experiencing God?

Father, I want to learn to pray. Teach me to concentrate
and see what You are doing to answer my prayer.
Thank You for the times recently when I have seen
You work in my life to answer prayer. Amen.

September 15

God Works As He Wills

He said to them, "Go, tell that fox, 'Behold, I cast out demons and perform cures today and tomorrow, and the third day I shall be perfected.'"

~ Luke 13:32

God is not our servant to make adjustment to our plans. We are His servants, and we adjust our lives to what He is about to do. If we will not submit, God will let us follow our own devices.

In following them, however, we will never experience what God is wanting to do through us for others. Even the king ("that fox") could not dictate Jesus' plans. Why do you try to?

Master Planner, You made the world, and You know how to fulfill Your purposes in it. Still, I try to take over the world and tell You how to run it. Forgive me. I place my plans in Your hands and wait for You to reveal Your plans, Your purposes and Your ways to me. Amen.

September 16

God Loves Prodigals

*"He arose and came to his father. But when he was still
a great way off, his father saw him and had compassion,
and ran and fell on his neck and kissed him."*

~ Luke 15:20

The prodigal son had to race around the world searching for what he had right at home. Our heavenly Father is on the look out for you, pursuing a love relationship with you. Are you running away so fast that you cannot see Him? What keeps you from accepting the Father's love?

*Loving Father, Your child is coming home. I have
been running away from You as fast as I could.
Forgive me. Take me back. I want nothing else but
a love relationship with You. Amen.*

September 17

Earthly Treasures

When Jesus heard these things, He said to him, "You still lack one thing. Sell all that you have and distribute to the poor, and you will have treasure in heaven; and come, follow Me."

~ Luke 18:22

God does not want to see you miss out on His best, so He has given you guidelines. This sounds good – until you start to apply them. They are tough. One guideline is to get rid of all things that tempt you to disobey God. Is treasure in heaven more important to you than treasure on earth?

You have blessed me with material goods, yet I keep on using all my money for things I really do not need. Show me how to know the difference between what I need and what I let the world tell me I need. Amen.

September 18

Know the Scriptures

*Then He took the twelve aside and said to them,
"Behold, we are going up to Jerusalem, and all things
that are written by the prophets concerning the
Son of Man will be accomplished."*

~ Luke 18:31

Jesus knew Scripture intimately. He repeatedly lived His life in light of what He had read in Scripture, even to the point of accepting a shameful death.

Are you willing to learn Scripture that intimately and follow it that closely? If so, you can be assured that God will speak to you through the Bible.

*Author of Scripture, I want to hear You speaking
to my situation. Even if You are leading me to
such a drastic step as sacrificial death for others,
I want to know it and live it out today. Amen.*

Believe the Resurrection

Then He said to them, "O foolish ones, and
slow of heart to believe in all that the prophets
have spoken. Ought not the Christ to have
suffered these things and to enter into His glory?"

~ Luke 24:25-26

One point in history brings all of us to a crisis of belief: That is the resurrection of Jesus Christ. Do you believe God raised Jesus from the dead? Does this belief change your life and the way you make decisions every day you live? This is not a one-time experience. It is a daily experience.

Resurrected Jesus, You have demonstrated to
us the power of God and the purpose of God.
I confess my faith in You as God's son. I have died to
sin and been raised to newness of life in You. Cause
that newness to show through to the world in every
decision I make and in every action I take. Amen.

September 20

Accepting Betrayal

"You will be betrayed even by parents and brothers,
relatives and friends; and they will put some of you to
death. And you will be hated by all for My name's sake."
~ Luke 21:16-17

Sometimes obedience to God's will leads to opposition and misunderstandings. Have you ever had an experience with God where your adjustment or obedience to God was very costly? What human relationships are you willing to sacrifice to remain loyal to God?

You mean more to me than any relationship
here on earth. Still, I have difficulty listening to
only You. You call me to a new kind of life, not
dependent on family and friends, but on You alone.
Be close so I can follow Your way. Amen.

September 21

Accepting Forgiveness

Then Jesus said, "Father, forgive them,
for they do not know what they do."

~ *Luke 23:34*

In your relationship with God, He may let you make a wrong decision. Then the Spirit of God causes you to recognize that it is not God's will and guides you back to the right path. He will even take the circumstance of your disobedience and work that together for good. This happens because He forgives you, even to the point of praying for you as He died on the cross. Can you accept His forgiveness and start over with Him?

Forgiveness is part of Your nature. You show how deep our love relationship is by forgiving the most grievous sins I commit. Give me the grace and freedom to accept forgiveness and forgive myself. Amen.

September 22

God's Eternal Word

The Word became flesh and dwelt among us,
and we beheld His glory, the glory as of the only
begotten of the Father, full of grace and truth.

~ John 1:14

Through Jesus, God Himself spoke to His people during His lifetime and Jesus is God's eternal Word. Now God speaks through the Holy Spirit. The Holy Spirit will teach you all things and will glorify Christ as He reveals Christ to you.

God's intention has always been to let people see, hear, and know Jesus. Has the Spirit led you to know Jesus? Is Jesus at work through you?

Eternal Word, speak to me now. Let me know what work You are doing in my world. Show me what I can do to join in that work and glorify You through it. Make my life reflect Your grace and truth. Amen.

September 23

An Intimate Love Relationship

"For God so loved the world that He gave His only begotten Son, that whoever believes in Him should not perish but have everlasting life."

~ *John 3:16*

God has drawn us to Himself. He sent His only Son to provide eternal life for you. This opened the way for a real love relationship between you and God.

Experiencing God depends on you having this relationship of love. He did all that is necessary for you to have this relationship. Do you have it?

Sacrificial Lamb of God, You died to give me eternal life. Nothing could show me any clearer how much You love me. God, I love You enough to obey You no matter what You ask me to do. Let me experience that intimate love relationship only You can create. Amen.

September 24

God Invites You
Through Christ's Example

Then Jesus answered and said to them, "Most assuredly,
I say to you, the Son can do nothing of Himself, but
what He sees the Father do; for whatever He does,
the Son also does in like manner."

~ John 5:19

How does God invite you to be involved with Him? Jesus' example shows you. You can do nothing apart from God. Because God loves you and wants to involve you in His work, He will show you everything so you can join Him. But you must watch to see where He is working.

Worker in my world, open my blind eyes. I see so much
activity around me but so seldom see You at work. Your
works should be so evident. Help me. I am watching.
I will see You at work. I will join You. Amen.

September 25

Do the Impossible

Then Jesus lifted up His eyes, and seeing a great multitude coming toward Him, He said to Philip, "Where shall we buy bread, that these may eat?" But this He said to test him, for He Himself knew what He would do.

~ *John 6:5-6*

I wonder if God ever tests our faith like He did Philip's. Does He say, "Feed the multitudes," and the church responds, "Our budget couldn't do it"?

Jesus as the Head of the church says, "I will never give you an order that I will not release My power to enable it to happen." Do you and your church have faith to believe that? Only then can God do God-sized work through you.

All-powerful God, You ask me to see only You as the certainty of the situation. Give me eyes of faith and a heart of courage to do the impossible with You. Amen.

September 26

Who Is He?

He answered and said, "Who is He, Lord,
that I may believe in Him?"

~ John 9:36

When God reveals what He has purposed to do, you face a crisis – a decision time. God and the world can tell from your response what you really believe about God.

The man born blind kept hunting for answers about Jesus. Jesus kept supplying them. The man believed and worshiped. The Pharisees refused to believe and remained dead in sin. How do you answer the all-crucial question, "Who is He?"

Jesus, You are Lord, Master, Savior, Son of God.
I fall and worship You. I rise to serve You. Point the
way so I may join Your work, obey Your Word,
and experience You. Amen.

Paying the Cost

From that time many of His disciples went back and walked with Him no more. Then Jesus said to the twelve, "Do you also want to go away?" But Simon Peter answered Him, "Lord, to whom shall we go? You have the words of eternal life."

~ John 6:66-68

Many people followed Jesus in the good times, but when trouble appeared on the horizon, they turned away. Jesus' true disciples saw no alternative.

Which group of disciples do you belong to, those who turn away at the sight of trouble, or those who are willing to pay the cost to do God's will?

Leader of the world, we choose to follow You. Business, family, personal dreams, may all disappear. That is a small price to pay for a love relationship with You. I will not turn away, no matter the cost. Amen.

September 28

The Great I Am

"I am the door. If anyone enters by Me, he will be saved, and will go in and out and find pasture. I have come that they may have life, and that they may have it more abundantly. I am the good shepherd. The good shepherd gives His life for the sheep."

~ John 10:9-11

To know and experience Jesus in these ways – the door to eternal life or the good shepherd who leads you to eternal life – requires that you believe in Him. When you believe in Him, adjust your life to Him, and obey Him. Come to experience Him.

Great I AM, thank You for opening the door to salvation. I do experience life, truth, and resurrection through You. How great You are! Amen.

God Works
Through the Spirit

"The Helper, the Holy Spirit, whom the Father will send in My name, He will teach you all things, and bring to your remembrance all things that I said to you."

~ *John 14:26*

God has not changed. He still speaks to His people. If you have trouble hearing God speak, you are in trouble at the very heart of your Christian experience. Jesus sent the Holy Spirit to live in your heart. There the Spirit communicates to you the things of God. Have you heard Him recently? Why not?

Holy Spirit, abide in me. Control my life.
Use the Bible, the church, circumstances,
and Your inner witness to let me know what God
is doing and how I can be a part of it. Amen.

September 30

October

He said to them, "Go into all the world and
preach the gospel to every creature. He who believes
and is baptized will be saved." ~ Mark 16:15-16

God Seeks Obedience

"He who has My commandments and keeps them, it is he who loves Me. And he who loves Me will be loved by My Father, and I will love him and manifest Myself to him."

~ *John 14:21*

God will call you to obey Him and do whatever He asks of you. However, you do not need to be doing something to feel fulfilled. You are fulfilled completely in a love relationship with God.

Why do you obey God? Are you trying to create a love relationship by being worthy of His love? You will never succeed. Or are you obeying because that is how you respond to God's love? That is a relationship of fulfillment.

Jesus, You do love me. You have shown this in so many ways. I know I cannot earn Your love, but I love You so much I do want to serve You obediently. Amen.

God Invites You
to Feed His Lambs

*When they had eaten breakfast, Jesus said to Simon
Peter, "Simon, son of Jonah, do you love Me more
than these?" He said to Him, "Yes, Lord; You know that
I love You." He said to him, "Feed My lambs."*

~ *John 21:15*

Some things only God can do. These include: drawing people to Himself; revealing spiritual truth; convicting the world of guilt regarding sin; convicting the world of judgment. When you see these things happening, you know God is at work and is inviting you to join Him. Do you see God at work? Do you help others see Him?

*Great Shepherd of the church, show me the work
You are doing now. Help me become mature
enough in You that I can help others grow so
they can also see You at work. Amen.*

October 2

God Speaks the Truth

Jesus said to him, "I am the way, the truth, and the life.
No one comes to the Father except through Me."

~ John 14:6

When the Holy Spirit talks to you, He is going to reveal Truth to you. You cannot know the truth of your circumstances until you have heard from God. What kind of truth do you seek? Is the Person who is Truth living in you?

O Truth, live in me. So often I am confused by
people interpreting life in so many ways. What I
need is the Truth and the Life living in me and giving
me Truth amid the circumstances. I seek You and
You alone to be my guide through life. Amen.

October 3

Searching for Proof

The other disciples therefore said to him, "We have seen the Lord." So he said to them, "Unless I see in His hands the print of the nails, and put my finger into the print of the nails, and put my hand into His side, I will not believe."

~ John 20:25

Thomas had plenty of witnesses who told him about the resurrected Jesus. But Thomas refused to believe. He demanded more proof. What kind of proof would make you believe in Jesus? Do you not have enough proof already in the work God is doing around you?

Risen Jesus, I praise You for giving me hope of eternal life through Your resurrection. You have done all I need to have faith. Help my unbelief. I will believe You today. Amen.

Paying the Price

When Jesus therefore saw His mother, and the disciple whom He loved standing by, He said to His mother, "Woman, behold your son!" Then He said to the disciple, "Behold your mother!"

~ John 14:26-27

When the Lord Jesus died on the cross, His obedience broke His mother's heart. His obedience put fear and pain in the lives of His disciples. For Jesus to do the will of God, others had to pay a high cost. If Jesus was willing to make life adjustments that cost Him and His loved ones so much, are you willing to do the same?

Suffering Lord, forgive me when I try to make excuses for avoiding the pain of obedience. I know some things I must do to adjust my life. I will make those adjustments no matter the cost. Amen.

Keeping God's Words

*"He who does not love Me does not keep
My words; and the word which you hear
is not Mine but the Father's who sent Me."*

~ *John 14:24*

Obedience is the outward expression of your love for God. If you have an obedience problem, you have a love problem. God is love. His will is always best. God is all knowing. His directions are always right. God is all powerful. He can enable you to do His will. If you love Him, you will obey Him. What kind of love do you really have?

*Eternal Word of God, come to my heart and
weld my love and my obedience together into
an inseparable package. I love You and want to
obey every Word You have given. Amen.*

October 6

God Gives Boldness
for Mission

When they saw the boldness of Peter and John, and perceived
that they were uneducated and untrained men, they marveled.
And they realized that they had been with Jesus.

~ Acts 4:13

None of the people God ever encountered could remain the same afterwards. They had to make major adjustments in their lives in order to walk obediently with God.

Two fishermen, Peter and John, became bold preachers in the cities of the world. What can you become if you place your life alongside God's activity?

Bold Mover of mountains, I know I do not have
the capability in my strength, but neither did Peter
and John. Help me stay God-centered so I may
always be in the center of Your work. Amen.

A Chosen Vessel

The Lord said to him, "Go, for he is a chosen vessel
of Mine to bear My name before Gentiles, kings, and
the children of Israel. For I will show him how many
things he must suffer for My name's sake."

~ Acts 9:15-16

When God came to Saul, Saul was actually fighting against Jesus. Jesus came to him and revealed the Father's purposes of love for him. We do not choose Him. He chooses us, loves us, and reveals His eternal purposes for our lives. What purposes has He revealed to you?

Lord of love, reveal Your purpose for my life.
I know you have chosen me for Your work but
help me see the pattern You are weaving with my life.
Thank You for choosing me even before I knew of
Your love. I love You. Amen.

October 8

Don't Doubt

While Peter thought about the vision, the Spirit said to him, "Behold, three men are seeking you. Arise therefore, go down and go with them, doubting nothing; for I have sent them."

~ Acts 10:19-20

God says that if He ever lets His people know what He is about to do, it is as good as done. He will bring it to pass. We have this assurance. Is your work with God plagued with doubts? Why? Are you sure you are doing what God has revealed to you? Or are you doing something you think it would be nice for God to do?

Spirit of the living God, speak to me. Show me where to go in Your work. Take away all fear and all doubt. Send me with bold certainty that I am a part of Your eternal work. Amen.

October 9

God Speaks to the Church

When they had prayed, the place where they were assembled
together was shaken; and they were all filled with the Holy
Spirit, and they spoke the word of God with boldness.

~ Acts 4:31

In the church's earliest beginnings, the Holy Spirit did not single out special individuals and come only to them. The Spirit came to all the members, giving all the power to interpret God's Word. Are you trying to be a lone ranger Christian when God wants you to work and learn within the fellowship of the church?

Holy Spirit, thank You for my local church, for the
many members who encourage me, teach me, train me,
and help me understand You, Your ways, and Your
purposes. Speak to our church. Amen.

October 10

The Door to God-Sized
Church Growth

Peter put them all out, and knelt down and prayed. And turning to the body he said, "Tabitha, arise." And she opened her eyes, and when she saw Peter she sat up. And it became known throughout all Joppa, and many believed on the Lord.

~ Acts 9:40, 42

Christians in the early church followed the directions of the Holy Spirit. When people saw God at work through His servants, God, not the servants, got the credit. Will you lead your church through its present crisis of belief so the world will see God at work?

Father, our church wants to do good, but we are not willing to let You have the credit. We trust only in our plans and activities and not in You. Help us through this crisis of belief so that we may experience You. Amen.

October 11

When Friends Suffer

When they did not find them, they dragged Jason and some brethren to the rulers of the city, crying out, "These who have turned the world upside down have come here too."

~ Acts 17:6

When Paul followed God's will, others were led to respond to God's work in their own lives. Jason and some other men were arrested by a rioting mob and accused of treason because of their association with Paul.

Frequently, Paul's obedience to God's will endangered the lives of others. Will you obey God even when it harms close friends?

Friend, I want to join You in the work. I also know the results for my closest earthly friends. I fear for them. Show me Your direction in this difficult decision. Amen.

October 12

God of the Open Door

When they had gone through Phrygia and the region
of Galatia, they were forbidden by the Holy Spirit to preach
the word in Asia. And a vision appeared to Paul in the night.
A man of Macedonia stood and pleaded with him, saying,
"Come over to Macedonia and help us."

~ Acts 16:6, 9

Paul was trying to figure out what he should do and the door of opportunity seemed to close. Actually, God was telling Paul to wait and He would show Paul what to do. Will you sit down with God and make sure you know what He has said to you?

God of the open door, oftentimes You seem to close doors
in my face. Show me anew the call You have given me
and what You want me to accomplish with You. Amen.

October 13

God Gives Salvation

*The wages of sin is death, but the gift of God
is eternal life in Christ Jesus our Lord.*

~ Romans 6:23

If you sense a need to accept Jesus as your Savior
and Lord, now is the time to settle this matter with
God. To place your faith in Jesus and receive His
gift of eternal life, you must: recognize that you are
a sinner and that you need a saving relationship
with Jesus; confess your sins; repent of your sins;
ask Jesus to save you by His grace, and let Him be
your Lord. Will you let God save you today?

*Savior, I have sinned against You. My life is far
from what You want it to be. Forgive me. I turn
from my sins. Please, Jesus, save me by Your grace.
Become King of all I am and hope to be. Amen.*

God Initiates a Love Relationship with You

As it is written: "There is none righteous, no, not one; there is none who understands; there is none who seeks after God. They have all turned aside; they have together become unprofitable; there is none who does good, no, not one."

~ Romans 3:10-12

Sin has affected us so deeply that no one seeks after God on his own initiative. If we are to have any relationship with Him or His Son, God will have to take the initiative. He is seeking a love relationship with You. Will you accept His gift of love?

God who seeks me, I want a love relationship with You. I want to know You in the most intimate, loving ways. I do love You, Lord. Amen.

October 15

God Invites You
to Be a Sacrifice

I beseech you therefore, brethren, by the mercies of God, that you present your bodies a living sacrifice, holy, acceptable to God, which is your reasonable service.

~ Romans 12:1

Obedience to God's invitation is never a simple matter. You take all that you are and give it to God, just as Israel took an entire animal and placed it on the altar as a sacrifice. Only such total commitment and obedience makes sense in God's perspective. Anything less is unacceptable. Are you doing the sensible thing in your relationship with God and His invitation?

Holy One, I come to You with nothing held back.
I am ready to do everything needed, sacrifice all
I am and all I have so that I may fully answer Your
invitation and join You in Your work. Amen.

October 16

God Speaks to Give Hope

Whatever things were written before were written for our learning, that we through the patience and comfort of the Scriptures might have hope.

~ Romans 15:4

God speaks to you through Scripture to help you be a person with hope. As you read the Bible, listen for words that bring comfort and hope to your life. Use these to help the church find hope as it praises God and to proclaim the Word of hope to the world.

Hope of the world, You have done all things possible to provide hope in a world that often seems so hopeless. Let me become an instrument of hope in my church and in my world. May the hope of Your Word shine through my life. Amen.

October 17

Sin or Salvation?

*What shall we say then? Shall we continue
in sin that grace may abound?*

~ Romans 6:1

The natural mind easily argues that it is to our advantage to sin. After all, grace comes to forgive sin. The more opportunity we give God to forgive sin, the more grace the world will receive.

Paul says such argument is absurd. No reasoning can justify sin. You must make a decision: sin or salvation, disobedience or obedience, no experience of God or experiencing God. Which decision will you make?

*God of grace, I am a sinner saved by Your grace
and called to obedience. The world uses so many
ways to convince me that sin is acceptable, even
necessary, or perhaps good in some cases. You tell
me sin is never good. I trust You. I reject sin.
You will be Lord of my life. Sin will not. Amen.*

October 18

Prayer

Likewise the Spirit also helps in our weaknesses. For
we do not know what we should pray for as we ought,
but the Spirit Himself makes intercession for us
with groanings which cannot be uttered.

~ Romans 8:26

The Holy Spirit guides you to pray according to God's will. Otherwise, you would pray according to self-centered human will. What prayer adjustments is the Spirit making in your life? How does that affect the way you obey God?

Spirit of God, teach me to pray. Take away
the last remnants of self will. Replace it
with Yourself so that Your will controls my
prayers, my actions, my attitudes, my desires, and
my relationships. Thank You, Holy Spirit. Amen.

October 19

Letting Christ Judge

*Why do you judge your brother? Or why do
you show contempt for your brother? For we shall
all stand before the judgment seat of Christ.*

~ *Romans 14:10*

You will experience God only as you take eyes off
the wrongs of other people and place eyes on the
work God is doing. Your confession of faith should
be: Lord, I will do anything that Your kingdom
requires of me; wherever You want me to be, I'll go;
whatever the circumstances, I'm willing to follow.

Is this your confession of faith to God, or are you
too busy telling other people what is wrong with
them to obey God?

*Christ, You are my judge. I resign my self-appointed
position as judge of the world. I will simply pray and do
anything the Kingdom requires. Amen.*

October 20

God Works Through Spiritual Gifts

There are diversities of gifts, but the same Spirit.
There are differences of ministries, but the same Lord.
And there are diversities of activities, but it is
the same God who works all in all.

~ 1 Corinthians 12:4-6

Self-centeredness causes us to see our God-given gifts and ministries as the best. Those lacking our gifts we may see as inferior. God-centeredness sees God doing His work according to His eternal plan through every one of His people, none being better than the other. God can only accomplish His purposes through us when we are God-centered.

Equipper of the saints, thank You for the spiritual gifts and the ministries You have given me. Give me the God-centeredness to focus on the work You are doing, not the gifts I have. Amen.

October 21

Quiet Time with God

The love of Christ compels us, because we judge thus:
that if One died for all, then all died; and He died for all,
that those who live should live no longer for themselves,
but for Him who died for them and rose again.

~ 2 Corinthians 5:14-15

I hear many people say, "I struggle to find time to be alone with God." If that is a problem you face, make the priority in your life to love God with all your heart. That will solve your problem with your quiet time. Love compelled Paul to be with Jesus. What are you compelled to do?

Why am I more compelled to watch sports than I am to be alone with You? Why do I want to play golf or go shopping more than I want to pray? Forgive me. I will spend time with You each day to love You more. Amen.

Seize the Day

He says: "In an acceptable time I have heard you, and in the day of salvation I have helped you." Behold, now is the accepted time; behold, now is the day of salvation.

~ 2 Corinthians 6:2

When God reveals to you what He is doing around you, that is your invitation to join Him. The Bible tells you that today is God's day of salvation. Whose fault is it that you do not see what God is doing?

Savior, I seize today as Your day. As You take the initiative in my life to open my eyes and show me what You are doing, I will join in. I will let today be Your day of salvation in my life. Amen.

God Speaks to You Through the Spirit

He who is spiritual judges all things, yet he himself is rightly judged by no one. For "who has known the mind of the Lord that he may instruct Him?" But we have the mind of Christ.

~ 1 Corinthians 2:15-16

On our own we cannot understand the truths of God. Aided by the Spirit, we can understand all things.

Do you know God, His purposes, and His ways? How have you learned them? Pray for the mind of Christ.

Holy Spirit, let the mind of Christ take over my heart and my soul. Show me Yourself, Your ways, Your purposes as I read Your Word. Amen.

October 24

A Crisis of Faith Requires God

My speech and my preaching were not with
persuasive words of human wisdom, but in demonstration
of the Spirit and of power, that your faith should not be
in the wisdom of men but in the power of God.

~ 1 Corinthians 2:4-5

On what should you base your faith? Have you become so confident in your own intelligence, reasoning, and persuasive skills that you no longer rely on God in times of crisis?

Your abilities can bring on a crisis of faith, forcing you to decide whether to depend on self or on God.

Author of our faith, too often I look inward to my own abilities when decisions face me. God, how can I leave You out of the decision-making process? Forgive me. Amen.

October 25

Following Christ's Example

You know the grace of our Lord Jesus Christ, that
though He was rich, yet for your sakes He became poor,
that you through His poverty might become rich.

~ 2 Corinthians 8:9

God even required major adjustments of His own
Son. Jesus emptied Himself of position in heaven
in order to join the Father in providing redemption
through His death on the cross – that was a major
adjustment. If Jesus was willing to adjust His life,
what adjustment can be too big for you to make?

Crucified One, You showed us Your humility and
love as You adjusted from heaven's glory to earth's
gore. Now You ask me to move, change jobs, take up a
new occupation, give up some comforts of life so
I can serve You. Your love compels me. I will make
these changes for You. I love You. Amen.

October 26

Give God the Glory

*Of Him you are in Christ Jesus, who became for us
wisdom from God – and righteousness and sanctification
and redemption – that, as it is written, "He who
glories, let him glory in the LORD."*

~ 1 Corinthians 1:30-31

If you are obedient, God will work some wonderful things through you. But you will need to be very careful that any testimony about what God has done only gives glory to Him. You will want to declare the wonderful deeds of the Lord, but you must avoid any sense of pride. Are you too proud of your religion, your duties at church, your accomplishments for God?

*My Glory, You deserve all praise, honor, and worship.
Help me find affirmation and love in You and not from
other sources. To God be the glory. Amen.*

October 27

God Calls You
to Proclaim Him

When it pleased God, who separated me from my mother's womb and called me through His grace, to reveal His Son in me, that I might preach Him among the Gentiles, I did not immediately confer with flesh and blood.

~ Galatians 1:15-16

God may want to work through you to impact others in your community. Are you so self-centered that you respond, "I don't think I am trained. I don't think I am able to do it"? God is working and wants to show you the part of His work He will enable you to accomplish.

God, You have called me to be a part of Your work. Make clear the work You are doing and the part I have in it. Then, we will work together. Amen.

October 28

God Gives Himself for Me

I have been crucified with Christ; it is no longer
I who live, but Christ lives in me; and the life which I
now live in the flesh I live by faith in the Son
of God, who loved me and gave Himself for me.

~ Galatians 2:20

If you knew that all you had was a relationship with God, would you be totally and completely satisfied? You know what Jesus has done for you. You know Jesus is available to live in you. You know that Christ wants the best for you. You know that Christ in you is the only way to eternal life. Do you still want more?

Inhabitant of my heart, be all that I want.
Calm my fears. Do away with my ambitions.
Soothe my anxieties. Nail all my selfish wishes to the
cross so that You alone are the center of all I want,
all I think, all I will, and all I do. Live in me. Amen.

October 29

Serve One Another

All the law is fulfilled in one word, even in this:
"You shall love your neighbor as yourself."

~ Galatians 5:14

God's work is always a work of love for others, not harm. God has told us that He is already at work trying to bring a lost world to Himself.

That revelation is His invitation to get us involved in His work, bringing others to a love relationship with God.

Author of freedom, I have the freedom to forget
self and serve others in love. I have the freedom
to love You and obey You out of that love. Amen.

Abba Father

*Because you are sons, God has sent forth the Spirit
of His Son into your hearts, crying out, "Abba, Father!"
Therefore you are no longer a slave but a son, and if
a son, then an heir of God through Christ.*

~ Galatians 4:6-7

When God accomplishes His purposes through us,
people will come to know God. His way is to make
you His child in the love relationship of parent/
child. Are you in a relationship with God so intimate
and close that you can call Him, "Daddy," and share
your heart with Him?

*Dearest Daddy in heaven, I feel so close to You
right now. I want to share with You the feelings
that flood my soul. Put Your strong arms around me.
Know that I love You. Amen.*

November

The fruit of the Spirit is love, joy, peace, longsuffering,
kindness, goodness, faithfulness, gentleness, self-control.
Against such there is no law. ~ Galatians 5:22-23

Which Gospel?

I marvel that you are turning away so soon from Him who called you in the grace of Christ to a different gospel, which is not another; but there are some who trouble you and want to pervert the gospel of Christ.

~ Galatians 1:6-7

God offers you a gospel of faith. The world offers good news at every corner, tempting you to come its way. Religious people show you the gospel without cost or obedience. You face a crisis of belief: which gospel do you follow?

Jesus Christ, only You offer a gospel that is truly good news. Others trick me into believing they have the magic solution for life's problems. Do not let me take the easy way out and try to find a gospel without a cross. Amen.

November 1

Restore the Fallen

*Brethren, if a man is overtaken in any trespass, you who
are spiritual restore such a one in a spirit of gentleness,
considering yourself lest you also be tempted.*

~ Galatians 6:1

Major adjustments come at the point of acting
on your faith. One area of adjustment is in your
relationships with others. Faith calls you to love
those who have missed God's mark in life, to love
them with such a great love that you help them up,
forgive them, and restore them to usefulness for
God. Have you adjusted your life to treat others
with forgiving, redeeming love?

*Gentle Jesus, give me Your gentleness of spirit so that
I may love the unloving and unlovely. Teach me to
love myself in such a way that I help others when they
are down rather than build myself up at their expense.
Show me how to restore them to You in love. Amen.*

November 2

The Fruits of the Spirit

*The fruit of the Spirit is love, joy, peace, longsuffering,
kindness, goodness, faithfulness, gentleness, self-control.
Against such there is no law. And those who are Christ's have
crucified the flesh with its passions and desires. If we live in
the Spirit, let us also walk in the Spirit.*

~ Galatians 5:22-25

The first step of obedience is to submit your life
to the Spirit of God in you. You will know this is
happening when the fruit of the Spirit appears in
your life. How would a spiritual fruit inspector
grade you?

*Spirit of God, manage my attitudes, my thoughts, my
habits, my prejudices until my life displays all the fruit of
the Spirit. This is the deepest desire of my heart. Amen.*

November 3

God Works His Possibilities

*To Him who is able to do exceedingly abundantly
above all that we ask or think, according to the power that
works in us, to Him be glory in the church by Jesus Christ
to all generations, forever and ever. Amen.*

~ Ephesians 3:20-21

Anything significant that happens in your life is a result of God's activity in your life. He is infinitely more interested in your life than you or I could possibly be.

Let the Spirit of God bring you into an intimate relationship with the God of the universe. Then see your possibilities of service multiply beyond your imagination.

*Lord of the universe, Your creative powers stretch
far beyond my wildest dreams and imaginations.
You have revealed to me that You want to unleash
such power in my life to accomplish Your work.
Do so, dear Lord. Do so today. Amen.*

November 4

God Makes Us Alive

God, who is rich in mercy, because of His great love with which He loved us, even when we were dead in trespasses, made us alive together with Christ (by grace you have been saved), and raised us up together, and made us sit together in the heavenly places in Christ Jesus.

~ Ephesians 2:4-6

God's kingdom purposes began when He decided to create a church out of sinners. The climax will be when the church is gathered in heaven to worship and love Him. Meanwhile, the church confesses that we have life only because God gave it to us in Christ. Are you alive in Christ or dead in trespasses?

Merciful God, what You have done in Christ cannot be described with human words. My response can be nothing else but wholehearted love for You. Amen.

November 5

Put on God's Armor

*Put on the whole armor of God, that you may be
able to stand against the wiles of the devil.*

~ Ephesians 6:11

To talk of a love relationship with God sounds good, but daily life turns out to be a grueling battle with evil. How do you prepare yourself for such a battle? Do you know the resources available to you in the fight? God invites you to put on the armor He provides for spiritual battle. Are you wearing it?

*Commander-in-chief, equip me for battle. Give
me Your truth, righteousness, peace, faith, salvation.
Yes, give me every piece of armor I need, and
I will be a loyal soldier for You. Amen.*

November 6

God Speaks Through the Church

Speaking the truth in love, may grow up in all things into Him who is the head – Christ – from whom the whole body, joined and knit together by what every joint supplies, according to the effective working by which every part does its share, causes growth of the body for the edifying of itself in love.

~ Ephesians 4:15-16

The church is the body of Christ. Every member is placed in the body as it pleases God. The Holy Spirit manifests Himself to every person, equipping them for kingdom work in unique ways. Therefore, we need each other. Have you found your place in Christ's body?

Head of the church, thank You for each member of my church and how they help me grow in Your love. Direct our church and select it for Your work. Amen.

November 7

Keep the Unity of the Spirit

*I, therefore, the prisoner of the Lord, beseech
you to walk worthy of the calling with which you
were called, with all lowliness and gentleness, with
longsuffering, bearing with one another in love, endeavoring
to keep the unity of the Spirit in the bond of peace.*

~ Ephesians 4:1-3

Church unity begins with each individual having a love relationship with God. It continues with all the members becoming rightly related to Jesus Christ as the Head of the church. How are you related to God, to the other members of His body? Do you promote unity or discord in the body?

*Holy Spirit, come unify Your church as You are in
unity with the Father and the Son. Bring us together
in love, in action, and in humility. Amen.*

November 8

Love As Christ Loved

Husbands, love your wives, just as Christ also loved the church and gave Himself for her, that He might sanctify and cleanse her with the washing of water by the word.

~ Ephesians 5:25-26

God has commanded you to love your family, especially your mate. This means adjusting your time schedule and your business plans to include quality time and quantity of time for the one you love. Love cannot always be expressed at long distance. Are you trying to do so?

Creator of families, I thank You for my family and the love with which they surround me. Forgive me when I take them and their love for granted. Work in me to get my priorities straight so I can truly love my family sacrificially as Christ loves me. Amen.

November 9

Redeeming the Time in Evil Days

See then that you walk circumspectly, not as fools but as wise, redeeming the time, because the days are evil.

~ Ephesians 5:15-16

Obedience is life's wise path, not its foolish one. Self-centered living is foolish and repels people who could be brought to God. Servant living attracts them to you and to the Lord you serve.

Obedient, servant living thus redeems each minute you live and gives you the opportunity to redeem that time for others. Does God think your time is redeemed?

*Redeemer of my life, time is the great resource
You have given me. How I use time shows who
I am and whom I love. Give me wisdom to use
my time that I may witness to You. Amen.*

November 10

God Works Through You for His Purpose

Therefore, my beloved, as you have always obeyed, not as in my presence only, but now much more in my absence, work out your own salvation with fear and trembling; for it is God who works in you both to will and to do for His good pleasure.

~ Philippians 2:12-13

Agree that: God is absolutely trustworthy; you will follow Him one day at a time, even when He does not spell out all the details; you will let Him be your way. If you cannot agree to these right now, openly confess your struggles to Him. Claim the promise that He will work in you to do His will.

*Worker of Your divine will, work in me.
I will follow Your way today even though I do
not know all the details involved. I know You
will work through me. Thank You. Amen.*

November 11

Created for Eternity

Not that I have already attained, or am already perfected;
but I press on, that I may lay hold of that for which Christ
Jesus has also laid hold of me. I press toward the goal for the
prize of the upward call of God in Christ Jesus.

~ Philippians 3:12, 14

Paul's real desire was to know Christ and become
like Him. You too can come to know Him, love Him,
and become like Christ. Let your present be molded
and shaped by what you are to become in Christ.
You were created for eternity!

Master of eternity, You have used the past to
shape me for the present. But You have created
me to live life eternal now. I press toward the
future in the hope of Christ. Amen.

November 12

God Invites You to
See the Finished Work

Being confident of this very thing, that He who has begun a good work in you will complete it until the day of Jesus Christ.
~ Philippians 1:6

God's invitation is not to a temporary, passing event. It is to a work that will be completed by the Master Workman and that will have results lasting into eternity. Do you want to be part of that kind of work? Answer God's invitation to join Him in His work.

Master Workman, You always complete what
You start. Today I hear Your invitation. I know
the work You are doing around me and I will
join in. I look forward expectantly to the day
You will show me the finished work. Amen.

November 13

God Speaks through His Churches

Now you Philippians know also that in the beginning of the gospel, when I departed from Macedonia, no church shared with me concerning giving and receiving but you only. For even in Thessalonica you sent aid once and again for my necessities.

~ Philippians 4:15-16

The churches of the New Testament helped and encouraged each other. As we experience this koinonia, or God's kind of fellowship, with other groups of God's people, we experience greater dimensions of God's presence at work in our world.

Lord of the church, thank You that You gave us other churches to teach and help us. Bless our family of churches around the world as You work through each of them. Amen.

November 14

Faith or Terror?

Only let your conduct be worthy of the gospel of Christ ...
that you stand fast in one spirit, with one mind striving
together for the faith of the gospel, and not in any way
terrified by your adversaries, which is to them a proof of
perdition, but to you of salvation, and that from God.

~ Philippians 1:27-28

Lack of faith often comes because you are "terrified by your adversaries." Such terror shows the world that people who claim to have faith are really weak.

Faith that stands against the world gives the world a clear alternative. Is your life a sign of worldly terror or godly faith?

Holy One, I want to act always fearing You, not the world. I promise today my commitment to a life that shows the world how much I love You. Amen.

November 15

Conformed to Christ

That I may know Him and the power of His resurrection, and
the fellowship of His sufferings, being conformed to His death,
if, by any means, I may attain to the resurrection from the dead.

~ *Philippians 3:10-11*

Because of his obedience, Paul suffered much for the
cause of Christ. Paul saw such suffering as sharing
in Christ's sufferings and dying to self and sin as
Christ had. Are you willing to share His sufferings
and to die to self and sin so you may experience the
resurrection?

Suffering Servant, give me the faith and
courage to persevere in suffering so I may win
the victory in resurrection. Amen.

November 16

The Mind of Christ

Let this mind be in you which was also in Christ Jesus, who, being in the form of God, did not consider it robbery to be equal with God, but made Himself of no reputation, taking the form of a bondservant, and coming in the likeness of men.

~ Philippians 2:5-7

Jesus came as a servant to accomplish God's will in the redemption of humanity. Does God want Jesus to be your model for life? Does He want you to be a servant? If you decide to obey God and become a servant, what must change in your life for you to obey and experience God?

Humble Servant, You left heaven where You were fully God and came to earth to be a servant of people like me. Give me the humility to be a servant like You. Amen.

November 17

Let God Mold You

He is the head of the body, the church, who is the
beginning, the firstborn from the dead, that in
all things He may have the preeminence.

~ Colossians 1:18

God established each church as a body of Christ, so
that He could continue His redemptive work in the
world. When Christ is allowed to function as Head
of His church, God can use the body to carry out
His will. Is your church working to show the entire
earth that Christ is the Head of all things?

Preeminent Lord of all the earth, mold Your church
to reflect You so that Your will may be carried out
throughout the world. O, image of the invisible God,
start the work of molding with me. Amen.

November 18

Forgiveness – God's Way

*Therefore, as the elect of God, holy and beloved, put
on tender mercies, kindness, humility, meekness,
longsuffering; bearing with one another, and forgiving
one another, if anyone has a complaint against another;
even as Christ forgave you, so you also must do.*

~ Colossians 3:12-13

The principles of God's Kingdom and the principles
of the world are vastly different. Are you devoted
to the world's way or to God's way that comes only
out of a love relationship with Him? How high are
you on the ladder of forgiving others?

*Forgiver of sins, teach me to forgive. Come into my heart
that I may be part of building Your Kingdom. Amen.*

November 19

Walk in Christ

As you therefore have received Christ Jesus the Lord,
so walk in Him, rooted and built up in Him and
established in the faith, as you have been taught,
abounding in it with thanksgiving.

~ Colossians 2:6-7

God has one basic commandment: walk in Christ. That means that your life is to become an image, a reflection of Christ's life. To walk in Christ shows that you are established in the faith and gives you reason to live each day giving thanks for what Christ is doing. Has God freed you to be like Christ, or are you still imprisoned by the world's ways?

You who make us free, we no longer find sin ruling
and dominating our lives. Now we can love You and
serve You, which is what we are created to do. Control
each step I take, each word I speak, each relationship
I form so that Christ shines in all. Amen.

November 20

God Makes the Riches Known

To them God willed to make known what are the riches
of the glory of this mystery among the Gentiles:
which is Christ in you, the hope of glory.

~ Colossians 1:27

We already know the overall plan God has: to let all people, Jews and Gentiles, know the riches of the Good News of Christ. What part has God given you in sharing the mystery? Do other people gain hope because You share Christ?

Hope of glory, show me where You are making known the riches of the glory of Christ in people You choose. Teach me to be Your spokesperson, letting others know the Good News of Jesus. Amen.

Reject Deceivers

*Now this I say lest anyone should
deceive you with persuasive words.*

~ Colossians 2:4

When God tells you what He wants to do, you will face a crisis of belief. Other people will have a different opinion and will express that opinion skillfully. You must decide: God's word or the word of other people? All eternity hangs on whether you choose God's way or human ways; on whether you find God's love relationship more appealing than human acceptance. Which appeals more to you?

Word of life, I cling to You. So many bring brilliant words, beautiful words, persuasive words, appealing words. But Your Word says they are deceivers, leading me down a false path that leads only to deception and death. Yes, I cling to You. I love You. Amen.

November 22

Sewn Together in Love

That their hearts may be encouraged, being knit together in love, and attaining to all riches of the full assurance of understanding, to the knowledge of the mystery of God, both of the Father and of Christ.

~ Colossians 2:2

God will reveal His plans and purposes, but obedience comes with a high cost. Paul repeated this message to the church as he suffered emotionally as well as physically.

He wanted his actions to be an encouragement, helping knit the church together in love. Are you willing to pay the emotional cost of adjusting your life to Christ and be an encouragement to other believers?

Father, I accept the suffering that will come because I want to join Your work. Let me be an agent of Your love. Amen.

November 23

Christ Is All in All

Do not lie to one another, since you have put off the old man with his deeds, and have put on the new man who is renewed in knowledge according to the image of Him who created him, where there is neither Greek nor Jew, circumcised nor uncircumcised, barbarian, Scythian, slave nor free, but Christ is all and in all.

~ Colossians 3:9-11

The New Testament gives you instructions that speak specifically to how God's people ought to live in relation to others. These instructions are written so you may know how to experience abundant life in Christ. Are you satisfied that you are living in Christ as you relate to other church members? Is Christ all in all?

My All in All, I do not object to any command You give. Open my heart that I may hear all You say. Amen.

November 24

God Guards You from Satan

*The Lord is faithful, who will establish
you and guard you from the evil one.*

~ 2 Thessalonians 3:3

God wants you to come to a greater knowledge of Him by experience. He faithfully works in your life, pursuing a love relationship with you.

Part of His work is protecting you from Satan so you can do His work. Can you relate an experience where you knew God was protecting you from the Evil One?

Faithful Protector, thank You. Daily I feel Your presence guiding my life in Your paths and setting up barriers against the attacks of Satan. Whatever I do is possible only because You are faithful and allow me to join in Your work. Thank You for Your faithfulness. Amen.

November 25

Abounding Love

*May the Lord make you increase and abound in love
to one another and to all, just as we do to you.*

~ 1 Thessalonians 3:12

You can experience God through relationships with other believers as He works in their lives. That is why we need each other. Since we were created to function as a body, we cannot be healthy apart from an intimate relationship with other believers. Is your love abounding for the other members of your church?

Lord of the church, You teach me so much through people in my church. Thank You for teachers who instructed me as a child, for deacons who showed me the meaning of loving service, for ministers who showed me how to delve deeply into Your Word, for class members who showed me the depths of prayer. Thank You for living through the people in our church. Amen.

November 26

Comfort One Another

Therefore comfort each other and edify
one another, just as you also are doing.

~ 1 Thessalonians 5:11

God wants to use you to strengthen His body by giving strength to other members of His body. You give them strength when you comfort them during times of hurt and when you teach them and build them up in times of growth. What gifts has God given you to help the church?

Comforter of my soul, use me to comfort
others. Give me a sensitive heart to understand
when others are in need. Give me confidence to
use the spiritual gifts You have given me in
ministry. Give me wisdom, love, and energy
to do the work even better. Amen.

November 27

God Speaks
through the Epistles

I charge you by the Lord that this epistle
be read to all the holy brethren.

~ 1 Thessalonians 5:27

When God leads you to a fresh understanding through Scripture: write down the verse; meditate on the verse; immerse yourself in the meaning of the verse; identify the adjustments you need to make so God can work that way with you; write a prayer response to God; watch to see how God may use that truth about Himself in your life today. Will you start or renew this kind of Bible study each day?

Inspirer of the Bible, give me Your presence as I
read Your Word. Teach me how to study it and
experience You as I read. Use Your Word to show
me the path to loving and obeying You. Amen.

November 28

Pursue Good

*See that no one renders evil for evil to anyone, but always
pursue what is good both for yourselves and for all.*

~ 1 Thessalonians 5:15

You cannot be in true fellowship with God and be out of fellowship with your fellow Christians. Thus, in every personal relationship, you face a crisis of belief.

Will you treat the other person in God's ways or in the way you feel at the moment? Are you treating someone with evil? How can you pursue what is good for them?

*Good One, You will never lead me to do evil
because You are good. Teach me the good ways.
You know the person I treat the worst. Change
my heart, and open the door for me to do good
for this person I have so mistreated. Amen.*

November 29

Work While You Wait

Even when we were with you, we commanded
you this: If anyone will not work, neither shall he eat.

~ 2 Thessalonians 3:10

The Thessalonians had become so convinced the end of the world was at hand that they quit secular and church work. Paul reminded them that working is part of God's creation and a responsibility for each one of us up until the moment Jesus comes again.

Is your work part of the stewardship you give to God and part of the love relationship you have with God?

Father, You showed us in creation how You are always at work. God, teach us to find in work the same meaning and hope that You find in Your work. Show me how my job fits into the love relationship I have with You. Amen.

December

"You shall know the truth, and the truth shall make you free." ~ John 8:32

Hold the Traditions

*Therefore, brethren, stand fast and hold the traditions
which you were taught, whether by word or our epistle.*

~ *2 Thessalonians 2:15*

The commands of Jesus come to you first through
the Scriptures, the basic tradition of the church. Any
new command you may receive for your life will
always be in line with Scripture. You will never find
truth that contradicts the way Jesus lived and the
way Jesus taught in the Bible.

*Jesus, be Lord of my life. Too often I have drifted
from one lifestyle to another, always seeking something
new. Today, I quit my search. I have found You in
Scripture. I need a love relationship with You that
allows and empowers me to do things Your way.
I am Yours. Teach me, Lord. Amen.*

December 1

God Grants Repentance

*A servant of the Lord must not quarrel but be gentle to all,
able to teach, patient, in humility correcting those who are
in opposition, if God perhaps will grant them repentance,
so that they may know the truth.*

~ 2 Timothy 2:24-25

When Christ is able to guide each spiritual leader and member of the body to function properly, the whole body will know and be enabled to do God's will. How are you working through your church to bring people away from quarreling to a way that God can lead them to repentance? Is God working repentance in your life?

Merciful God, help our church be Your agent of repentance in our community. Work in my life to bring repentance where You see it is necessary. Amen.

December 2

God's Love for the Church

Greet those who love us in the faith.
Grace be with you all. Amen.

~ Titus 3:15

Members of a church are interdependent on one another and need each other. The church creates a body in love relationship, which reflects the love relationship God has with each individual.

Church leaders away from the body send greetings back to it in love and concern as Paul did. Do you experience this kind of love relationship in your church?

Creator of the church, thank You for bringing together into this one body such a warm fellowship of love and concern. Help me to always be grateful for the members of our church and for the loving support I get from them. Help me give them the love You so richly give me. Amen.

December 3

Pray for Everyone

Therefore I exhort first of all that supplications, prayers, intercessions, and giving of thanks be made for all men, for kings and all who are in authority, that we may lead a quiet and peaceable life in all godliness and reverence.

~ 1 Timothy 2:1-2

God can touch a world through you. God invites you to pray for all people, especially for people who make important world decisions. How does the world missions prayer strategy of your church affect world leaders?

Universal Lord, work through our leaders, even when they are not in a love relationship with You, to create Your good purposes on our earth. Show me how to pray and how to work to bring Your purposes to pass. Amen.

December 4

God Speaks Through Inspired Scripture

All Scripture is given by inspiration of God, and is profitable for doctrine, for reproof, for correction, for instruction in righteousness, that the man of God may be complete, thoroughly equipped for every good work,

~ 2 Timothy 3:16-17

Your task is to wait until the Master gives you instructions. Are you reading the God-breathed instruction book that reveals Him to you? Or are you so anxious to get to work that you ignore the instruction book? Without Bible reading, you are ill-equipped for living.

Source of all inspiration, I thank You for the Bible and the Truth You reveal through it. I dedicate myself to reading it and finding Your will before I step out on my own. Amen.

December 5

How to Grow in Christ

*The things that you have heard from me among
many witnesses, commit these to faithful men who
will be able to teach others also.*

~ 2 Timothy 2:2

No one can become the kind of complete believer you ought to be outside the functioning body of a New Testament church. Why? Because God has placed the discipling process in the body of the church. Are you trying to grow in Christ by yourself? You need to find a body of Christ that will teach you the faith.

*Great Teacher, minister to me. I seek to grow
in Your grace, but I cannot do it by myself.
Show me how to function in Your body so I can
grow. Thank You now for the teachers You have
provided and will provide to help me. Amen.*

December 6

Endure for Christ

Therefore I endure all things for the sake of the elect,
that they also may obtain the salvation which is
in Christ Jesus with eternal glory.

~ 2 Timothy 2:10

You may think of waiting as a passive, inactive time, but waiting on the Lord is anything but inactive. While you wait on Him, pray with a passion to know Him; watch circumstances and ask God to interpret them; share with other believers to find out what God is saying to them.

Your endurance brings others to know Christ's salvation.

Eternal Savior, I want to see immediate results.
But You are testing my faith and making me wait
for signals You give to move. Give me patience.
Help me to be a servant for others as I wait for You. Amen.

December 7

Put God First

Command those who are rich in this present age not
to be haughty, nor to trust in uncertain riches but in the
living God, who gives us richly all things to enjoy.

~ 1 Timothy 6:17

The Holy Spirit will guide you daily to the specific commands He wants you to obey. Perhaps the command today is to place Him above your money and property. Do you truly have more trust in God than in your possessions?

Giver of every good and perfect gift, take away
all signs of pride from my life that would
prevent me from being Your servant. I want to
find joy in You and You alone. Amen.

December 8

God Works in Different Ways

God, who at various times and in various ways spoke in time past to the fathers by the prophets, has in these last days spoken to us by His Son, whom He has appointed heir of all things, through whom also He made the worlds.

~ Hebrews 1:1-2

In the Old Testament God spoke at many times and in a variety of ways. Through Jesus, God Himself spoke to His people during His lifetime. Now God speaks through the Holy Spirit. Are you listening for His voice?

Spirit, speak. Let me see You at work and let me know how to join in Your work. Thank You that You have always come to us and spoken to Your people. Amen.

Breaking Down Barriers

Perhaps he departed for a while for this purpose, that you might receive him forever, no longer as a slave but more than a slave – a beloved brother, especially to me but how much more to you, both in the flesh and in the Lord.

~ Philemon 15-16

God wants members of His church to love one another, because the world will know that we are His disciples by our love. Paul faced Philemon with a major question about his love relationship with God. Did he love God enough to love a disobedient slave? How is God testing your love for Him?

Master of all, help me show mercy to those around me, not because I should be a merciful master, but because I should be a merciful servant. Amen.

December 10

Throw Sin Away
and Run the Race

*Therefore we also, since we are surrounded by so great
a cloud of witnesses, let us lay aside every weight, and the
sin which so easily ensnares us, and let us run with
endurance the race that is set before us.*

~ Hebrews 12:1

Hebrews invites you to take heart from all the faithful believers who have prepared the path for you, to throw away everything that would delay or entrap you, and to run as fast and as hard as you can with Christ. Do you accept the invitation?

Coach, push me past my meager limitations. Help increase my endurance through training and dedication to Your Word. Thank You for the example of the great spiritual athletes who have come before me. May I measure up to the standards they have set. Amen.

December 11

Piercing Your Life

The word of God is living and powerful, and sharper than any two-edged sword, piercing even to the division of soul and spirit, and of joints and marrow, and is a discerner of the thoughts and intents of the heart.

~ Hebrews 4:12

God uses Scripture as a sharp sword to cut to the core and show adjustments you need to make so that nothing hinders you from a love relationship with Him. He may do this through one Bible verse which convicts you of the working of the Holy Spirit. Will you listen as God speaks and make the changes He calls for?

Discipline is Your work. Your Spirit uses the Bible to judge my life and show me where I fall short of Your goals. I cry out for help in overcoming my sin and coming back to You. Amen.

December 12

Pleasing God

*Without faith it is impossible to please Him, for he who
comes to God must believe that He is, and that He is a
rewarder of those who diligently seek Him.*

~ *Hebrews 11:6*

If you or your church are not responding to God
or attempting things that only He can accomplish,
then you are not exercising faith. If people in your
community are not responding to the gospel like
you see in the New Testament, one possible reason
is that they are not seeing God in what you are
doing as a church.

*Doer of the impossible, forgive my lack of faith. Help
me to quit relying on my own resources and start
having the faith to find what You are doing and rely
on Your plans and Your resources. Amen.*

December 13

Hold Fast the Confession

Let us hold fast the confession of our hope
without wavering, for He who promised is faithful.

~ Hebrews 10:23

When God encounters you, you need to learn how to pray – and that will require major adjustments. You may need to let God wake you up in the middle of the night to pray or you may even pray all night. Do you have enough confidence in God to adjust your prayer life?

Listener to every word I pray, make my life devoted to prayer, worship, Kingdom work, and helping others to participate in the love relationship with You. Amen.

December 14

God Disciplines in Love

You have forgotten the exhortation which speaks
to you as to sons: "My son, do not despise the chastening
of the Lord, nor be discouraged when you are rebuked
by Him; for whom the Lord loves He chastens,
and scourges every son whom He receives."

~ Hebrews 12:5-6

God's discipline is a form of love, designed to draw us back into fellowship with Him. Fellowship with God is the most cherished privilege of the child of God and He may withdraw His presence out of need for discipline. Are you in fellowship with Him, or are you experiencing His discipline?

Loving Father, You punish because You love.
Bring us to our knees in repentance. Restore us to
that wonderful love relationship that only You
can make possible. Amen.

December 15

God Works Through Ordinary People

Elijah was a man with a nature like ours, and he prayed earnestly that it would not rain; and it did not rain on the land for three years and six months. And he prayed again, and the heaven gave rain, and the earth produced its fruit.

~ James 5:17-18

Elijah was an ordinary man just like we are ordinary. He prayed and God responded. God is able to do anything He pleases with one ordinary person fully consecrated to Him. Are you that person who will pray and do God's work like Elijah?

User of ordinary people, use me. Whatever gifts, talents, skills, resources You have given me, I give back to You. Use me, Lord, to do the impossible, God-sized tasks You are up to right now. Thank You, Lord. Amen.

December 16

God Is Love

Whoever confesses that Jesus is the Son of God, God abides in him, and he in God. And we have known and believed the love that God has for us. God is love, and he who abides in love abides in God, and God in him.

~ 1 John 4:15-16

By believing in Jesus, we have eternal life. The Father will love us. He will make us more than conquerors over all difficulties.

We never will be separated from His love. God loved us first and His very nature is love. Have you believed in Jesus and experienced the love that is God Himself?

Love, pure, unprejudiced, divine Love, come to me. Let me feel Your strong arms around me. I believe in You. I will make my home in You. Make Your home in me so that the whole world may see Your love. Amen.

December 17

God Invites
You to Holiness

As He who called you is holy, you also be holy in all your conduct, because it is written, "Be holy, for I am holy."

~ 1 Peter 1:15-16

Throughout the New Testament, God expresses some of His desires for the church. God wants His people to be holy and pure. God wants His people to display unity. God wants His people to love each other. How would you evaluate your church's faithfulness to these commands? Is your church holy, pure, united, and loving?

O Holy One, Your holiness makes me drop to my knees in awe, in reverence, and in fear. I worship You because You are so different from anything I can ever be. Yet You invite me to be holy. What an awesome task! Make me holy. Amen.

December 18

Tuned in to the Spirit

*Knowing this first, that no prophecy of Scripture
is of any private interpretation, for prophecy never
came by the will of man, but holy men of God spoke
as they were moved by the Holy Spirit.*

~ 2 Peter 1:20-21

God speaks to you through the Bible. But a person cannot understand spiritual truth unless the Spirit of God reveals it.

Are you and your church studying God's Word together to see what the Holy Spirit wants to say to you today? Are you acting on what He says?

Spirit of the living God, breathe on us. Use the Holy Word to speak to my life. Make me attune to the Spirit so He can fit me into Your plans. Amen.

December 19

What Are You
Showing to the World?

Certain men have crept in unnoticed, who long ago were marked out for this condemnation, ungodly men, who turn the grace of our God into lewdness and deny the only Lord God and our Lord Jesus Christ.

~ Jude 4

The world will respond to the Christ they see in a life, a family, or a church. Two opinions will always attract you. One laughs at God, and says Jesus was a good teacher but not God in the flesh. The other raises Jesus up and shows the ways of God still working today. Which one does your life show the world?

Unique God, give me the Spirit of truth to ward off those who would tempt me to quit following You. Show the world Your power and Your truth through me. Amen.

December 20

Imitating the Good

*Beloved, do not imitate what is evil, but what is good. He who
does good is of God, but he who does evil has not seen God.*

~ 3 John 11

When you are willing to surrender everything in
your life to the lordship of Christ, you will find
that the adjustments are well worth the reward of
experiencing God.

If you have not come to the place in your life
where you have surrendered all to His lordship, decide today to deny yourself, take up your cross, and
follow Him.

*Good One, You have shown us in the person of Jesus
what it means to be good here on earth. Let me take no
lesser example. Take out Your repair tools and make me
over until I am Thine, doing the things You do, thinking
the things You think, loving the people You love. Amen.*

December 21

Abide in the Doctrine of Christ

Whoever transgresses and does not abide in the doctrine of Christ does not have God. He who abides in the doctrine of Christ has both the Father and the Son.

~ 2 John 9

When God gives you Ten Commandments, do you obey them? When Jesus tells you to love your enemies, do you love them? When Jesus tells your church to make disciples, do you obey Him? When God tells you to live in unity with your fellow Christians, do you?

You always need to learn more about Christian teaching, but the important question is, are you living out the doctrine you already know?

Master Teacher, help me to always believe the Truth of Christ Jesus and obey His teaching. Live in me as Your teaching lives through me. Amen.

December 22

God Works to
Rule the World

To Him who loved us and washed us from our sins in His
own blood, and has made us kings and priests to His God and
Father, to Him be glory and dominion forever and ever. Amen.

~ Revelation 1:5-6

Christians are kingdom people, and Christ Himself is the eternal King over His kingdom. In this partnership with Christ as King, you become involved in His mission to reconcile a lost world to God. You cannot be in relationship with Jesus and not be on mission. In what way are You on mission with Christ?

King of my life and of the universe, place me where
You want me to be. Open opportunities to work where
You are working. Fill me with Your Spirit so I can
reveal You to people who do not know You. I love You
and will do whatever You say. Amen.

December 23

Standing at the Door

"Behold, I stand at the door and knock. If anyone hears My voice and opens the door, I will come in to him and dine with him, and he with Me."

~ *Revelation 3:20*

God had something in mind when He called you. He began to work in your life. He began to open your understanding and drew you to Himself. He continues to invite you to enjoy that love relationship. Are you participating in it with zeal, or must you endure His discipline and repent?

Lover of my life, You pursued me, found me, and created a marvelous love relationship with me. Lord, continue to do everything necessary to maintain this love relationship. Amen.

December 24

God Is Faithful and True

Now I saw heaven opened, and behold, a white horse.
And He who sat on him was called Faithful and True,
and in righteousness He judges and makes war.

~ Revelation 19:11

Frequently in the Bible, when God revealed Himself to a person, the person gave God a new name or described Him in a new way.

Do you see that you have come to know God through experience? Has He been Faithful and True in your experience? What other names has your experience given God?

Faithful and True, we have experienced
You so many times as the only One who is faithful
to the word spoken and faithful to me in a true
love relationship. Help me to reflect to the world
Your faithfulness and Your truth. Amen.

December 25

Stay with Your First Love

"Nevertheless I have this against you, that you have left your first love. Remember therefore from where you have fallen; repent and do the first works, or else I will come to you quickly and remove your lampstand from its place – unless you repent."

~ Revelation 2:4-5

Living in faithful obedience to Him allows you to experience His presence. This is koinonia with God and you must know the essentials: love God with our total being, submit to God's sovereign rule, experience God in a real and personal way, and trust completely in God. Does this describe your relationship with God, or have you left your first love?

Lord of all fellowship, I want You to rule every minute of my life, every action I take, every thought I have, every relationship I enter into. Amen.

December 26

Is He Coming?

*"Behold, I am coming quickly! Blessed is he who keeps
the words of the prophecy of this book."*

~ *Revelation 22:7*

Christianity makes two quite unique claims. (1) The
Lord died and was resurrected from the dead, as-
cending into heaven. (2) The resurrected, ascended
Lord will come again.

The world laughs at such claims. The church
proclaims these are the greatest moments of the
world's experience. These counterclaims put you
in a crisis of belief. Do you believe Jesus rose? Do
you believe He is coming? Do you believe strongly
enough to obey what is in the Book?

*Risen, ascended, coming Lord, You live in my
heart. I know You are coming again. I experience
Your blessing as I keep Your Word. Come quickly,
Lord Jesus. Come in victory. Amen.*

December 27

No Stray Dog

*Blessed are those who do His commandments, that
they may have the right to the tree of life, and may
enter through the gates into the city. But outside are dogs
and sorcerers and sexually immoral and murderers and
idolaters, and whoever loves and practices a lie.*

~ Revelation 22:14-15

Life adjustment to God can be defined simply: do
His commandments. This includes the command-
ments written in the Bible, but also the ones the
Holy Spirit lays out before you each day. When
He comes, will you be inside the city with Him or
outside with the lying dogs?

*Source of life, I look forward to entering Your gates and
enjoying the tree of life with You. Don't let me become a
stray dog. I cleave to You and You alone. Amen.*

December 28

Inherit All Things

*"He who overcomes shall inherit all things, and I
will be his God and he shall be My son."*

~ *Revelation 21:7*

Experiencing God leads to a final victory. As His
child, You inherit everything He has. You will live
with Him in heaven through all eternity as joint heir
with Jesus. Is this the future you look forward to
and know you will experience?

*Father, I am Your child. I look forward to
inheritance day with You. Meanwhile, give me
the joy of the love relationship here on earth no
matter what it demands of me. Amen.*

God Works to Redeem a Lost World

Jesus said to them again, "Peace to you! As the Father has sent Me, I also send you."

~ John 20:21

Once Jesus returned to heaven, God fashioned a new body of Christ through the Holy Spirit. This body is the believers whom God has added to the church. God is at work all over the world building His kingdom. He sends members of His body everywhere He is at work. Where is He sending you to join in His work? Are you set to go?

Working, saving, redeeming God, You have placed me as a member of Your body, the church. You have created a love relationship with me and with our church. That relationship is not static and unchanging. It is dynamic and fruitful. Use me in Your kingdom work of redeeming this lost world. Amen.

December 30

A Relationship of Obedience and Experience

If we walk in the light as He is in the light, we have
fellowship with one another, and the blood of Jesus Christ
His Son cleanses us from all sin.

~ 1 John 1:7

God created us for koinonia, the fullest possible fellowship with Him. You cannot be in koinonia with God and not walk in godly fellowship with one another. Are you experiencing koinonia with God and with the church? You can.

Lord, You have pursued a love relationship
with me and invited me to join in Your work.
You spoke to me through Your Word and I faced the
crisis of belief. I am making the needed adjustments
so I can join in Your work. Now I am obeying You and
experiencing You. I love You. Amen.

December 31